Producing Bri

Ruth McElroy · Caitriona Noonan

Producing British Television Drama

Local Production in a Global Era

Ruth McElroy
Creative Industries
University of South Wales
Cardiff, UK

Caitriona Noonan
School of Journalism, Media
and Culture
Cardiff University
Cardiff, UK

ISBN 978-1-349-84603-0   ISBN 978-1-137-57875-4   (eBook)
https://doi.org/10.1057/978-1-137-57875-4

This Palgrave Macmillan imprint is published by the registered company Springer Nature Limited
The registered company address is: The Campus, 4 Crinan Street, London, N1 9XW, United Kingdom

ACKNOWLEDGEMENTS

This book is very much born from conversations with colleagues in The Centre for the Study of Media and Culture in Small Nations. They have supported this research by providing a productive space to discuss the challenges facing media in small nations. We wish to thank Emeritus Professor Steve Blandford who initially led the research team examining the BBC's Roath Lock Drama Studios and we are grateful to the Creative Industries Research Institute at the University of South Wales for funding that project.

We are grateful to the UK Arts and Humanities Research Council for funding our international research network, 'Television in Small Nations' (AH/M011348/1), and latterly an Early Career Research grant for 'Screen Agencies as Cultural Intermediaries: Negotiating and Shaping Cultural Policy for the Film and TV Industries within Selected Small Nations' (AH/R005591/1). More information about both projects can be found at www.smallnationsscreen.org. The authors also wish to acknowledge the Higher Education Funding Council for Wales who provided funding for research through their Strategic Insight Partnership programme.

We wish to acknowledge the feedback and generous help given to us by colleagues as we prepared the manuscript including Tom Ware, Susan Wood, Stephen Lacey, Simon Cottle and Karin Wahl Jorgensen. Colleagues on the 'What Makes Danish TV Travel?' team at Aarhus University have been hugely supportive through many active collaborations and conversations. Our thanks also to the two expert reviewers who provided constructive advice on the manuscript.

Much of the material included in this book was gleaned from interviews and discussions with those working within the television industry in the UK and elsewhere. We wish to thank the many industry collaborators and interviewees that have given so generously of their time to help inform our analysis and shape our contributions to the sector.

Finally, our thanks to family, friends and colleagues who supported us so graciously as we brought this book to life.

CONTENTS

LIST OF TABLES

CHAPTER 1

Introduction

Abstract This book is a critical response to a moment of profound change in the production and distribution of television drama. Drama content is central to the strategic aspirations of broadcasters, independent production companies and policy-makers helping them to deliver on a range of economic, cultural and political goals. Our analysis foregrounds power and sustainability as two significant terms that merit sustained critique and which underpin contemporary television drama production. This chapter outlines the novel methodological approaches adopted when conducting the many years of original empirical research with television drama professionals which underpins this book's contribution to the field. We offer a rich and in-depth analysis of contemporary television drama production in the UK, merging global and transnational trends with the enduring significance and value of local production.

Keywords Television drama · Production · Distribution · Public service broadcasting · Empirical research · Sustainability · Value

This book critically interrogates a key moment of change focusing on how the processes of commissioning, producing and distributing drama content are evolving. It provides readers with original, empirically grounded insight into the factors driving this evolution and focuses on the UK as a major supplier of, and market for, television drama. This is a significant moment in the restructuring of television production as

© The Author(s) 2019   1
R. McElroy and C. Noonan, *Producing British Television Drama*,
https://doi.org/10.1057/978-1-137-57875-4_1

critical discussions continue about the future of European models of public service broadcasting, technological innovation alters audience consumption patterns and greater competition comes in the form of new incumbents. This book is a critical response to this moment. While the forces of globalisation undoubtedly influence television production, we recognise local and global as two ingredients in this mix. It is the mobility, not only of texts, but also of policies, professional practices, and workers across local, national and global territories that resonate clearly and so throughout this book we attend to these different levels. While these processes are often alluded to, they are not consistently documented at the grass roots level of television production, nor are they always followed through in terms of how they impact on what we see on screen. Therefore, this book presents an intervention into scholarly debates by analysing the challenges and opportunities of making television drama in specific national and regional contexts. It critically analyses the specific set of conditions which impact on television drama's production at a local level and it argues for the value of attending to these conditions in the current digital era.

Our approach is informed by a sense of urgency and crisis in the midst of what is more commonly being framed as a 'golden age' of unparalleled abundance. Undoubtedly, a rich compendium of drama is being delivered by recent entrants such as Netflix, Hulu and Amazon Prime, but we eschew reading this as evidence of a sustainable pipeline of television drama production. Instead we assess holistically the broad ecology of television drama production and identify features of stress and erosion that we believe threaten the diversity and sustainability of this ecology. These areas of stress and erosion reflect the prevalence of neoliberal formations of market value, globalisation and deregulation in contemporary television production. Over the past decade or so, television drama has been transformed from a poor relation of Hollywood film to become a transnational phenomenon in its own right. As a corrective to the celebratory discourses of the 'era of abundance' and the 'golden age', we offer a richer, situated analysis of the precarity of the current ecology of drama production including the public service broadcasters and labour markets that sustain it. Without television drama, there would be a far inferior television service, be that from the subscription video on-demand (SVoD) suppliers or from longstanding public service broadcasters such as the BBC and ITV.

The Significance of Local Production

We advocate for the significance of local production in a global era of digital television. Television drama production has become an increasingly global business ranging from transnational content providers to multi-territory rights deals. However, a focus on international markets and global players can eclipse a deeper understanding of the material realities of who makes television drama. This book presents a compelling case for a paradigmatic shift towards centering the sustainability of local production in our understanding of how the current disruptions are shaping the sector. Like many of those working in and researching this sector, we attempt to make sense of a rapidly changing media environment in which the global and the local are in a dynamic and evolving relationship. This relationship is economic in character as new markets emerge for local content, and at the same time global players enter local production ecologies. However, we argue that there are overarching public values at stake within local production ecologies that go to the specific cultural and social significance of television drama.

Here we pause a moment to distinguish between *local production* and *local drama*. While both may overlap they are conceptually distinct. Take for instance the case of the highly successful drama *Sherlock* (2010–2017). While *Sherlock* is made in Cardiff, the series' fictional location is London, including the iconic 221B Baker Street, home to the eponymous detective. Frequently what appears on screen as London is in fact Cardiff. For example, in series two, episode three 'The Reichenbach Fall', scenes that are presented narratively as taking place in the Tower of London were actually shot in the far more accessible Cardiff Castle. Equally, our case study in Chapter 6, *Game of Thrones* (2011–2019), showcases much of the Northern Irish landscape as part of its filming in the region. Undoubtedly, both productions provide significant job opportunities for the local creative workforce and the opportunity for Cardiff and Northern Ireland to be seen on screens around the world. However, neither series tells viewers about the history or identity of the place or portrays the lives of those living there through their stories. Contemporary drama production renders places simultaneously visible and invisible, and as our research attests, this matters to viewers and local television professionals.

Therefore, throughout this book we argue for the value of *both* local production *and* local drama in a global era. Investment, jobs and indigenous business growth all mean that local production can matter financially for the places that can secure and develop this activity. But dramas which speak to the experiences and identities of those who inhabit a place also matter. Audiences want to see representations that are authentic and reflect their world. For the cultural and linguistic preservation of communities, television drama's communicative power is vital for the cultural and linguistic preservation of communities. We further contend that these localising elements hold the potential to enhance the market value of content, including in international markets. Numerous examples speak to the value of regional and local markers, including *Y Gwyll/Hinterland* (2015–present) and *Happy Valley* (2014–present), challenging the idea that local drama from the UK cannot travel. Indeed, television drama which speaks to the unique character of British identity can be core to the country's global visibility and is seen in the success of exports such as *Downton Abbey* (2010–2015), *Vera* (2011–present) and *Peaky Blinders* (2013–present) Some of this dual significance of local drama production is captured in this speech from Tony Hall, Director General of the BBC:

> [P]rogrammes that are rooted very clearly in specific communities around the UK don't just speak to us more directly, or help us understand more about ourselves. Shows like *The Fall* in Northern Ireland, *Shetland* in Scotland or *Hinterland* in Wales, do so much more for our nations. They act as magnets for ideas and talent, help find and develop local voices, and generate new jobs and investment. That's why the centres for drama production that the BBC has in Glasgow, Belfast and Cardiff are such an important part of the story of what the BBC does for Britain as a whole. (Hall 2017)

Here Hall positions the role of public service broadcasters, (hereafter PSBs) in relation to the provision of local production and local drama before warning about the risks to the latter from Amazon and Netflix whose investment decisions are based on content which can have international appeal. Therefore, the significance of local production lies not only in its economic value, but in its potential to create local dramas that imaginatively reflect our communities at home and to others. Throughout this book, we insist that the cultural value of television drama cannot be divorced from the policy and production conditions from which it emerges.

Our empirical research on the local production ecology for television drama reveals two key interlinked and enduring concerns within the television landscape: power and sustainability. This book argues for a renewed political approach to television drama production that re-centres questions of power in the analysis of whose stories are made and how they do, or do not, arrive on our screens. Power is distributed unevenly in the value chain of television drama. The sheer scale and resources of larger broadcasters and global media conglomerates makes for a highly unequal set of power relations that directly impacts on what viewers see on screen. While these forms of institutional power are a concern, we are also acutely aware of their relationship to cultural representation, scale and language. Stewart (2016) reminds us that the myth of televisual ubiquity obscures the role still played by national borders, cultural geographies and strategic business decisions such as geoblocking and windowing. Equally, English is still commonly seen as the 'language of advantage' (Collins 1989) when it comes to the global TV marketplace and this is one reason for the dominance of Anglophile TV content on European television screens. This is despite the growth of television that speaks from varied international experiences, most vividly seen in the influx of Nordic Noir to UK screens both on the BBC and Channel 4, but also in the use of tropes by British producers such as those involved in the Welsh crime dramas *Y Gwyll/Hinterland* and *Craith/Hidden* (2018–present).

We also argue for greater critical engagement with questions of sustainability within television drama production. Television drama research which focusses on individual high-end series or from major global showrunners tends not to concern itself with sustainability, nor with the security and longevity of the labour market from which it comes. However, sustainability has become a powerful framework for conceptualising the activities of the television sector. For instance, as one of the most lucrative and labour-intensive forms to produce, drama has become increasingly visible to policy-makers who are also concerned with the sustainability of their communities, its citizens and workers. Whether it be *Game of Thrones* filmed in Northern Ireland, *Outlander* (2014–present) in Scotland or *His Dark Materials* (2019–present) in Wales, there is considerable economic value in attracting inward investment from large-scale, high-end international productions, something that had previously been the preserve of film. As a result, television drama production has now become integral to the sustainability agendas of regional and national governments, public bodies, and cultural intermediaries such as screen funds and tourism agencies.

For these bodies, sustainability is often understood solely in economic terms. However, we argue that sustainability has applicability beyond economic concerns alone. As we outline in Table 1.1, sustainability can usefully be interpreted in cultural, industrial, technological and ecological terms. These interpretations are accompanied by a range of metrics and associated levers, which are employed by different stakeholders to diverse ends. These different interpretations of sustainability co-exist in the contemporary production landscape and so it is through this more nuanced conceptualisation of sustainability that the full non-economic value of television drama can be understood. Nurturing a sustainable ecology in all its forms requires holistic capacity-building for diverse drama markets nationally and internationally. Regulators and policy makers, as much as broadcasters, production companies, screen agencies and trade unions have a role to play in this endeavour. Consequently, their activity needs more consistently to inform scholarly understanding of television drama. Greater precision with the term allows for more effective policy interventions and more critical scholarship.

As we outline in the next chapter, drama content offers important commercial and cultural value which is vital to the sustainability of broadcasters—both commercially funded and those with a public service remit. Indeed, there is growing pressure on public service broadcasters to remain well-resourced and well-supported sources of substantial new and original television drama. However, we regard the erosion of public funding and the accelerating marketisation of public service broadcasting as a source of significant threat to the ecology. This book demonstrates how and why public service broadcasters remain the most important actors in this ecology and why their fate is our best guide to the sustainability of this ecology overall.

TELEVISION DRAMA AS FORM

Drama is an imaginative form that can invoke critical thinking, exploration and pleasure. The depth of engagement it can command distinguishes it from other forms of television. It provides a space to reflect, both subjectively and collectively, on wider social experiences in our changing world. Television drama is also a hugely elastic, embracing form. It is diverse in its format, from weekly soap operas to complex serial dramas, from returning series to the anthology. A range of genres including crime, medical, youth, historical and sci-fi elicit the passion

Table 1.1 Forms of sustainability in national and regional television production

	Economic	Cultural and social	Technological	Industrial	Labour	Environmental
Interpretation	TV sector contributes consistently to economic growth of nation/region	TV content contributes to cultural representation and enhances public good	Technical innovations deliver market returns	TV industry will grow and be resilient to change	Diverse, skilled workforce available to deliver range of content over long careers	Reduced environmental impact of TV production
Indicators	• Contribution to Gross Domestic Product (GDP) • High level of inward investment • Substantial multiplier effect[a] • Cross-sectoral spend (e.g. tourism) • High-value jobs & high rates of employment • High level of exports • International nation branding • High levels of capital investment • Indigenous business growth • Talent attraction and concentration of expertise	• Diverse & plural media forms • Critical mass of quality representations • Prominence and vitality of national and regional languages • Contributes to public debate • Contributes to plural, cohesive sense of national identities • Speaks to and from entire audience with diverse stories • Make-up of TV workforce reflects social composition of the wider population	• Monetisable Intellectual Property (IP) rights and patents • Growing demand from consumer and/or commercial markets • Entry into new markets • Adaptable technical infrastructure (e.g. 5G) • R&D infrastructure supports innovation	• Plurality of buyers (broadcasters/distributors) and suppliers (indies) • Diverse indigenous indies with growth capacity able to develop and retain IP across platforms • Appropriate levels of funding and support for PSBs • High levels of spend on original commissions and returning series' • High levels of inward investment • Competitive and complete supply chain (e.g. post-production) • Revenue-generating exports • Ability to leverage monetisable ancillary rights • Diverse and plentiful talent pool • Pipeline of emerging projects • Reputation for expertise	• Diverse and appropriately skilled labour market • Access to 'Above the Line' talent • Appropriate 'Below the Line'/ crew capacity • High rates of employment in the sector throughout the year (a 'pipeline of work') • Flexible and mobile workforce • Diverse workforce with high levels of access and participation • Low levels of attrition	• Reduced carbon footprint from activities like travel, set construction and location shooting • Use of local companies for supply chain • Encouraging audience engagement with ecological issues

(continued)

Table 1.1 (continued)

	Economic	Cultural and social	Technological	Industrial	Labour	Environmental
Examples of Political, Regulatory & Industry levers	• High-end television tax relief • Business development funding • Skills development and apprenticeship schemes • City Region Deals	• Public funding and support of diverse PSBs • Regulatory support for PSB • Regulatory quotas (e.g. Made Out of London) • Content development funding • Funding of archives • Reporting and accountability systems (e.g. regional spend) • Industry access schemes to overcome barriers to entry	• Copyright frameworks • Public investment in R&D infrastructure and support • Business development funding	• Sector investment (e.g. Welsh Government's Media Investment Budget) • Infrastructure investment • High-end television tax relief • Public funding of PSBs • Regulatory quotas (e.g. Out of London spend) • Seedcorn funding (e.g. Sky Vision fund; Channel 4 Alpha Fund)	• Access to appropriate education and training (e.g. screen agency skills programmes) • Welfare system and career support for freelancers and new entrants • Reporting and accountability systems (e.g. Project Diamond) • Inclusive PSB training schemes	• Albert certification scheme (http://wearealbert.org/)

[a]The multiplier measures the level an economy will grow following a change in the level of investment. A multiplier of two would mean that for every one pound spent, the economy would grow by two pounds. Multipliers are widely used in the television and film industries to measure the contribution of filming to a local economy. For instance, research shows that every pound of direct expenditure made in Aberystwyth as a result of filming *Y Gwyll/Hinterland* generated an additional spend of 57p in the local economy (IWA 2015, 38)

(and sometimes ire) of audiences. The core of television drama is its capacity to tell stories that appeal to a wide and diverse range of viewers, and it continues to win high ratings despite fragmenting audiences. For example, *Call the Midwife* (2012–present) and *Doctor Who* (2005–present) were among the most watched programmes on UK television on Christmas Day 2017, testifying to the enduring popularity of family drama and to the centrality of public service broadcasters to the range of dramas available. However, television drama's consistent appearance in weekly schedules and on-demand platforms around the world belies both the risky nature of its production and the invisible hands within that process who bear much of that risk. It is because of this complexity that we adopt the approach we do.

The significance of this book is its ability to empirically ground the analysis of disruption as it plays out in a particular place and moment. This allows for a more holistically, grounded view of how television drama emerges from and lives within specific locales. This approach necessitates reaching beyond the literature on television drama alone and extending into adjacent subjects including production studies, creative economy research, media policy and studies of cultural labour. We bring a cultural focus to bear on the analysis of local production ecologies. In doing so we evidence how complex relations of power are evolving and impacting the pipeline of what gets made where and by whom. In drawing together fields of enquiry that often do not speak to one another, this book advances and deepens the insights of television scholars into the ecology of drama production.

There has been renewed attention from television scholars to the political economy of television and to the associated corporate strategies which often place drama content at its core (e.g. Johnson 2019; Lobato 2019; Lotz 2014). Furthermore, changing audience behaviours for drama (e.g. bingeing) confront fundamental concepts such as flow and liveness which have specific implications for producers (Dhoest and Nele 2016; Holt and Sanson 2014). Television scholars are also paying more attention to the mobility of drama and its routes into new national and transnational markets (Hills et al. 2019; McCabe and Akass 2012; Waade et al. forthcoming) along with the specific dynamics of its production (Hammett-Jamart et al 2018; Raats et al. 2016; Redvall 2013). Drama has been an important anchor in that work due to its strategic value—something we expand on in the next chapter.

Our concern with television drama's cultural value means that we see substantial value in scholarship that attends to more textual accounts of the form and its evolution. There is a well-established body of work that attends to the value of television drama for audiences and critiques the forms of cultural representation on screen (Bignell and Lacey 2014; Cooke 2003; Forrest and Johnson 2017; Nelson 2007; Thornham and Purvis 2005). The flourishing of 'quality tv' scholarship emerges within this to reiterate the strategic and creative value of content like *The West Wing* (1999–2006), *The Sopranos* (1999–2007), *Life on Mars* (2006–2007) and *Spooks* (2002–2011) (Chapman forthcoming; Lacey and McElroy 2012; McCabe 2012; McCabe and Akass 2007; Polan 2009). More recently there has been vibrant scholarship on the aesthetic elements that make drama distinctive and on the complex forms of seriality and narrative that have developed (see Dunleavy 2009, 2017; Mittell 2015; Toft Hansen and Waade 2017). There is also a crucial literature which attends to the generic conventions of drama, especially in relation to crime (Lamb 2019; McElroy 2017; Piper 2015; Turnbull 2014).

Our research draws on and advances this scholarship. We provide a more holistic view of TV production by focusing on the range of drama's stakeholders to understand how TV is valued and mobilised by a more encompassing range of stakeholders such as policy-makers and cultural intermediaries. While others begin with the individual dramas' content or a specific aspect of production (e.g. screenwriting) to anchor their analysis, we begin with the context bringing together the people, institutions, places and policy, which are key components in the realisation of drama content, as they negotiate the dynamics of a global industry. This enables a richer and more robust understanding of the relationship of television drama to its publics, especially at a local level. The voices of these various stakeholders and a holistic understanding of their reality is central to our empirical research. This also demands an innovative methodological approach.

EMBEDDED METHODOLOGIES

The intellectual context from which our analyses of television drama have emerged has been shaped by a concern with the place of television in national and cultural politics. This book emerges from a programme of original, empirical research conducted over several years by the present authors alongside colleagues based at the Centre for Media and Culture in Small Nations at the University of South Wales.[1] The knowledge gathered from each individual project was cumulative, with findings from early projects directly informing subsequent research questions and methods, thereby enhancing the rigour and validity of the programme of research.[2] As we've argued elsewhere (McElroy et al. 2018), television scholars need to think innovatively about the range of formal research methods employed, but also the value (and risks) of sustained expert engagements with industry, policy-makers and regulators. We concur with Amanda Lotz (2015) that media industry research 'does not require dogmatic adherence to a particular tradition or outlook' but rather that such scholarship should draw from 'a vast toolkit of techniques for inquiry'.

Much of the texture of this research has been shaped by conducting investigations in Cardiff. Cardiff is one of the fastest-growing centres of drama production in the UK. As mentioned above by Tony Hall, the BBC has invested in the city as its centre of excellence for drama production. It is from the Cardiff area that some of the UK's most

---

[1] The Centre for the Study of Media and Culture in Small Nations coordinates research on the creative industries in Wales through the frame of small nations globally. For more information see http://culture.research.southwales.ac.uk/.

[2] The first phase of the research presented here was semi-structured interviews conducted in South Wales and Bristol in 2013 with eighteen key stakeholders, including staff at the main public service broadcasters (BBC and S4C), the Welsh Government's Creative Industries Department, independent producers, Creative Skillset, the trade union BECTU, and local screen development agencies. A number of follow-up discussions with our interviewees in the intervening years allowed us to refine and develop our thinking. In 2014 Noonan was awarded funding for a Strategic Insight Partnership by the Higher Education Funding Council for Wales to investigate collaboration and best practice in the Danish screen industries. During a secondment to the Øresund Film Commission in Copenhagen she carried out five interviews with key stakeholders and undertook a week of ethnographic research at the commission. A further source of data was through exchanges gathered at our AHRC funded international network on 'Television in Small Nations' (AH/M011348/1), a collaborative project between the authors, and industry partners including TG4, S4C and the European Broadcasting Union. The workshops in 2015–2016, involved both formal presentations and informal discussions and were recorded and transcribed with permission of participants. In attendance were approximately 63 participants from 12 countries. A final dataset emerges from 'Screen Agencies as Cultural Intermediaries: Negotiating and Shaping Cultural Policy for the Film and TV Industries within Selected Small Nations', our most recent research collaboration funded by the AHRC (AH/R005591/1). At the time of writing, interviews with the CEO and outgoing Chair of Ffilm Cymru, the screen agency of Wales had been conducted. It is this combined dataset, gathered in English and Welsh, that underpins the analysis in this book.

prestigious exports emanate including the BBC's *Doctor Who* (2005–present), *Sherlock* (2010–2017), Netflix's *Sex Education* (2019–present) and Sky's *A Discovery of Witches* (2018–present). Consequently, Wales offers an illuminating case study in which to anchor critical discussions of local production in a global era. Equally, the case of Northern Ireland offers a compelling context in which to observe and critique some of the dynamics of contemporary production, in part evidenced by the success of both global juggernaut *Game of Thrones* and the home-grown comedy *Derry Girls* (2018–present). Our location in Wales, a small European nation, has given us an opportunity to build sustained relationships with a diverse array of production professionals and to share critical inquiry and findings with local policy makers.[3] This location outside the mainstream established global centres of production affords the research a unique standpoint.

This book is also the embodiment of three overarching values we believe are central to cultivating media research which is meaningful both within and beyond academia. Firstly, our approach to methodology combines macro 'master' narratives of media production with the micro and everyday experiences of those engaged in, and associated with, drama production. Using interviews, in particular, we give voice to plural interests and perspectives. For example, in our earlier research 'Screening the Nation' (Blandford et al. 2010) with the BBC Trust and Audience Council Wales there was an explicit goal to understand audiences, especially those who are marginalised. This was followed by a study in 2013–2015 which captured the voice of workers embedded in and orbiting the new BBC studios in Roath Lock, Cardiff (McElroy and Noonan 2015). But rather than privilege senior decision-makers, our research included interviews with independent production companies, freelancers and new workers (such as apprentices) to hear from those who may have concerns which are fundamentally at odds with those of large institutions. It also captured voices beyond those of the traditional gatekeepers such as the trade union BECTU.

---

[3] Evidence of this knowledge exchange can be seen in the recent inquiry on 'Film and Major Television in Wales' conducted by the Culture, Welsh Language and Communications Committee of the National Assembly for Wales to which both authors submitted written and subsequently by invitation, oral evidence to the committee (National Assembly for Wales 2018).

Commitment to this diversity is important because it provides a fuller understanding of the material experience of making television drama. This approach demands a longer-term commitment to engaging with industry professionals across their own career stages and at different moments in the television industry's evolution. Methodologically, it is research which takes time; insights are drawn not solely from formal hour-long interviews, for example, but over many months and years of informal dialogue and engagement. Participating in the ecology we document is undoubtedly demanding but it rewards us as researchers with the kind of extensive data that could not be captured in shorter-term fieldwork alone.

A second value in our research agenda is our commitment to participatory knowledge exchange. This is best exemplified by our funding by the Arts and Humanities Research Council (AHRC) in 2015 for a project which was founded on this ethos and simultaneously extended the international scope of our analysis. Working closely with a research team at Aarhus University, who were themselves asking 'what makes Danish TV travel?' (http://danishtvdrama.au.dk/), our project was centred around convening a network of stakeholders to share their perspective on the challenges and changes facing television drama producers today. This project was multinational, multi-sited and multi-method but based on the principles of knowledge exchange. While a growing volume of academic research foregrounds professional perspectives, our objective in the network was to engage with industry practitioners as collaborators. Consequently, we organised a series of workshops formulated to ensure less demarcation between the researcher and the researched. This enabled us to achieve a more authentic and dialogic engagement between industry and academic professionals and contributed to often informal forms of knowledge exchange which themselves have considerable value as a route to impact.

While participants in the network came from different perspectives and different small nations, they coalesced around a common agenda and a commitment which exceeded professional success alone. They shared a common concern about the sustainability of drama production in the small nations in which they lived and worked, together with a socio-cultural commitment to hearing a diversity of local stories often in non-Anglophone languages. Their participation was rooted in a conception of small nations as primarily a category of power rather than of geographic or population size. Their work and ours brought into focus how questions of power and scale are integral to cultural production (McElroy and Noonan 2015, 2016; McElroy et al. 2018). We are assured of both the economic and cultural value of television drama that resonated in the voices of our interviewees. We observed an enduring cultural commitment to making 'good' drama against the backdrop of an economic reality that does not always support that ambition.

The sharing of best practice between participants across different small nations was part of our efforts to counter 'the menace of instrumentalism' (Hesmondhalgh 2014) in media industries research. Problems, sources and alternatives were core to discussions and we lend our weight to calls for a more nuanced understanding of knowledge exchange between academia and other spheres (Munro 2016; Belfiore 2016). Our legitimacy as autonomous researchers remained intact because of our expertise and our insistence on posing longer-term critical questions, while openness and trust were crucial to our research endeavours and to the continuing access we enjoy. Through the years of our research, we have negotiated—often with great tension as well as pleasure—different subject positionings as we argue alongside industry colleagues about the significance of any individual element of these disruptions. We are convinced that these embedded conversations have actually afforded us a greater sense of our own distinct contribution as scholars who—unlike many industry commentators—are able to withdraw from the immediate field to enjoy something of more holistic, analytical view of the myriad forces shaping any individual instance of disruption in the production ecology.

A third value emanates from this and relates to our active engagement in the policy process. This has taken myriad forms including providing expert evidence to DCMS,[4] Parliamentary[5] and National Assembly of Wales[6]

[4]Department for Digital, Culture Media & Sport: Building an S4C for the future: An independent review by Euryn Ogwen Williams (2018). Available at https://www.gov.uk/government/publications/building-an-s4c-for-the-future-an-independent-review-by-euryn-ogwen-williams.

[5]Parliamentary Welsh Affairs Committee Inquiry into Welsh Broadcasting (2016). Accessible online at https://www.parliamentlive.tv/Event/Index/35119192-b824-4bda-ae5d-d3f19aedbef5.

[6]Community Equality, and Local Government Committee, National Assembly for Wales, Inquiry into the BBC Charter Review (2016). Accessible online at http://www.senedd.assembly.wales/mgIssueHistoryHome.aspx?IId=13600.

Culture, Welsh-language and Communication Committee, National Assembly for Wales, Inquiry into the Future of S4C (2017). Accessible online at http://www.senedd.tv/Meeting/Archive/2dc561d2-e552-42dd-92fd-6cfa5edb8440?autostart=True#.

inquiries into different aspects of broadcasting, BBC Charter renewal, and high-end television drama production. In our research design, we have become increasingly aware of developing research with the potential to intervene directly in normative questions of what television drama should be now and in the future. Television drama's place within creative industries has often been invisible, though more recently has gained greater prominence as policy-makers acknowledge the multiple forms of value it can deliver. However, calcified modes of thinking among creative economy policy-makers and the gamut of other experts involved in this area has meant little critical thought internally (Schlesinger 2016). Our experiences of engaging publicly in debate with industry, politicians and regulators around building a culturally and economically sustainable industry suggests that while technology is often seen as a major instigator of change, other changes are equally disruptive. These include political change (such as devolution in the UK[7] and of course 'Brexit'); commercial changes to the revenue streams of independent production companies when supplying global players such as Netflix; regulatory changes (for example, the evolution of quotas for production outside London as well as diversity measures both on screen and off), and institutional change (notably BBC Charter review, the review of S4C, the Welsh-language public service broadcaster, and the relocation of Channel 4 out of London to a new Leeds headquarters and hubs in Bristol and Glasgow). Moreover, as *teachers* we are acutely conscious of the necessity of developing a more equitable and responsive talent pipeline that can be matched by a sustainable pipeline of commissions for workers throughout their careers.

ABOUT THIS BOOK

This book begins by outlining the specific value of drama to different stakeholders in order to offer a holistic analysis of British TV drama production. We engage with the rhetoric on the second 'golden age' of television drama, acknowledging its persuasive power within industry

---

[7] In the United Kingdom, devolution refers to the statutory granting of powers from the UK Parliament in Westminster to the Scottish Parliament, the National Assembly for Wales, and the Northern Ireland Assembly. Their associated executive bodies (the Scottish Government, the Welsh Government, and the Northern Ireland Executive) have different levels of legislative, administrative and budgetary autonomy.

discourse. Compared to other televisual forms, drama enjoys unique prominence and accrues myriad forms of value. We argue that greater precision is required in identifying how drama matters in economic, socio-cultural and political terms. By interrogating questions of value, we reveal how power and sustainability underpin the renewed prominence of television drama on our screens.

Having identified television drama's multiple forms of value, Chapter 3 details the process of producing that content in the UK today. It demystifies the production process from commissioning through to production and distribution, and in the process outlines some of the distinctive characteristics of UK TV. Chief among these characteristics is the relationship between PSBs as commissioners and the British independent production sector as suppliers, both of whom are responding to a more export-driven and on-demand production ecology in which the power of major global firms is being consolidated.

The power of drama lies in its imaginative capacity to tell the story of people and places. While textual analyses of television drama acknowledge this also, our research demonstrates that questions of cultural and professional identity are also integral to television drama production. In Chapter 4, we demonstrate how the appearance of certain places on screen, both as part of the narrative or as anonymous shooting locales, is not a matter of mere happenstance but is the product of myriad policy, regulatory and creative features, as a well as the material outcome of the flows of global capital. Regionality is a peculiar historic and contemporary characteristic of UK production. Moreover, it has a particular purchase for regulators and broadcasters who have specific targets for moving production out of London. Devolution in the UK since the 1990s has meant that questions of national representation and the broadcasters' response to this have enjoyed renewed public policy attention. It is by focusing on local production in particular that the impact of the global and digital era can be empirically traced.

The BBC's Roath Lock drama studios opened in Cardiff in 2012 and house a number of major productions including *Doctor Who*. We use Chapter 5 as a situated case study for understanding what it is like to work within British TV drama production. Increased internationalisation and deregulation of the TV industry has meant many specialist production crews work under precarious conditions often in short-term projects. A focus on a national broadcaster's investment in this studio reveals the potential value for regions and nations of building their own production labour market, as well as revealing the challenges to making this inherently risky sector sustainable.

Evidence of attempts to build a sustainable, local production ecology is also found in Northern Ireland, through its investment in *Game of Thrones*. In Chapter 6, we extend further the lens of local production to analyse the crucial role played by nationally funded cultural intermediaries in sustaining the value chain for television production. The chapter insists that cultural intermediaries such as screen commissions and regional tourist boards, play a significant role in seeking to actualise value from TV drama for their own policy agendas despite this role being frequently neglected in television drama scholarship.

The concluding chapter restates the case for urgent and profound attention be paid to power and sustainability within television drama scholarship. We argue for the necessity of a viable and invigorated public service media to emerge from this moment of disruption. This is not a moment for complacency on the part of broadcasters, producers or regulators. Concerns with the wider public good lie at the heart of pressing concerns such as the prominence and discoverability of content, the regulation of global media firms and the necessity to make drama a space for genuine—and often challenging—public debate. These are some of the ongoing struggles for power that will characterise the television landscape in the future.

Writing about the production of contemporary television drama carries with it the occupational hazard of being eclipsed by the seemingly endless supply of new dramas about to appear on our small screens. As we write this Introduction, we, like many other viewers, look forward eagerly to a new season of original drama productions. We wonder how Sally Wainwright will render the Brontë sisters, how Philip Pullman's *His Dark Materials* will appear on screen, and how US actor Rob Lowe will inhabit his role as a Lincolnshire police chief constable in *Wild Bill*. In arguing for a deeper and more critical assessment of the ecology, sustainability and diversity of television drama production we are eager to share our passion for the form and for the conversations and attachment it affords viewers as well as policy-makers and professionals. We hope the stories we tell here as researchers will substantially deepen our colleagues' and students' appreciation of television drama and the cultural, linguistic and economic value of this hugely diverse and innovative narrative form.

REFERENCES

Belfiore, Eleonora. 'Cultural Policy Research in the Real World: Curating "Impact", Facilitating "Enlightenment"'. *Cultural Trends* 25, 3 (2016): 205–216.

Bignell, Jonathan and Stephen Lacey (eds). *British Television Drama: Past, Present and Future*. 2nd edition. Basingstoke: Palgrave Macmillan, 2014.

Blandford, Steve, Stephen Lacey, Ruth McElroy and Rebecca Williams. 'Screening the Nation: Wales and Landmark Television', Report for the BBC Trust/Audience Council Wales, 2010. http://culture.research.southwales.ac.uk/screeningthenation/.

Chapman, James. *Contemporary British Television Drama*. I.B. Tauris, forthcoming.

Collins, Richard. 'The Language of Advantage: Satellite Television Is Western Europe'. *Media, Culture and Society* 11, 3 (1989): 351–371.

Cooke, Lez. *British Television Drama: A History*. London: British Film Institute, 2003.

Dhoest, Alexander and Nele, Simons. 'Still 'Watching' TV? The Consumption of TV Fiction by Engaged Audiences'. *Media and Communication* 4, 3 (2016): 176–184.

Dunleavy, Trisha. *Complex Serial Drama and Multiplatform Television*. New York: Routledge, 2017.

Dunleavy, Trisha. *Television Drama: Form, Agency, Innovation*. New York: Palgrave Macmillan, 2009.

Forrest, David and Beth Johnson (eds). *Social Class and Television Drama in Contemporary Britain*. Basingstoke: Palgrave Macmillan, 2017.

Hall, Tony. The Roscoe Lecture. Liverpool John Moores University, Thursday 2 November 2017. https://www.bbc.co.uk/mediacentre/speeches/2017/tony-hall-roscoe.

Hammett-Jamart, Julia, Petar Mitric and Eva Novrup Redvall (eds). *European Film and Television Co-production: Policy and Practice*. Basingstoke: Palgrave Macmillan, 2018.

Hesmondhalgh, David. 'The Menace of Instrumentalism in Media Industries Research and Education'. *Media Industries* 1, 1 (2014). http://dx.doi.org/10.3998/mij.15031809.0001.105.

Holt, Jennifer and Kevin Sanson (eds). *Connected Viewing: Selling, Streaming and Haring Media in the Digital Era*. London: Routledge, 2014.

Hills, Matt, Michele Hilmes and Roberta Pearson (eds). *Transatlantic Television Drama: Industries, Programs, and Fans*. Oxford: Oxford University Press, 2019.

IWA. *Wales Media Audit 2015*. Accessed 8 March 2019. https://www.iwa.wales/news/2015/11/iwa-wales-media-audit-2015/.

Johnson, Catherine. *Online TV.* Oxon: Routledge, 2019.

Lacey, Stephen and Ruth McElroy (eds). *Life on Mars: From Manchester to New York.* Cardiff: University of Wales Press, 2012.

Lamb, Ben. *You're Nicked: A History of the British Television Police Series, 1955 to Today.* Manchester: Manchester University Press, 2019.

Lobato, Ramon. *Netflix Nations: The Geography of Digital Distribution.* New York: New York University Press, 2019.

Lotz, Amanda. *The Television Will Be Revolutionized.* 2nd edition. New York: New York University Press, 2014.

Lotz, Amanda. 'Assembling a Toolkit'. *Media Industries* 1, 3 (2015). http://dx.doi.org/10.3998/mij.15031809.0001.304.

McCabe, Janet. *The West Wing.* Detroit: Wayne State University Press, 2012.

McCabe, Janet and Kim Akass (eds). *Quality TV: Contemporary American Television and Beyond.* London: I.B. Tauris, 2007.

McCabe, Janet and Kim Akass (eds). *TV's Betty Goes Global: From Telenovela to International Brand.* London: I.B. Tauris, 2012.

McElroy, Ruth. (ed) *Contemporary British Television Crime Drama: Cops on the Box.* London: Routledge, 2017.

McElroy, Ruth and Caitriona Noonan. 'Television Drama Production in Wales: BBC Wales. Roath Lock Studios. A Report by the Centre for the Study of Media and Culture in Small Nations, 2015. http://culture.research.southwales.ac.uk/roathlockdrama/.

McElroy, Ruth and Caitriona Noonan. 'Television Drama Production in Small Nations: Mobilities in a Changing Ecology'. *Journal of Popular Television* 4, 1 (2016): 109–127.

McElroy, Ruth, Caitriona Noonan and Jakob Isak Nielsen. 'Small Is Beautiful? The Salience of Scale and Power to Three European Cultures of TV Production'. *Critical Studies in Television* 13, 2 (2018): 169–187.

Mittell, Jason. *Complex TV: The Poetics of Contemporary Television Storytelling.* New York: New York University Press, 2015.

Munro, Ealasaid. 'Illuminating the Practice of Knowledge Exchange as a 'Pathway to Impact' Within an Arts and Humanities Research Council 'Creative Economy Knowledge Exchange' Project'. *Geoforum* 71, May (2016): 44–51. http://dx.doi.org/10.1016/j.geoforum.2016.03.002.

National Assembly for Wales. 'Film and Major Television Production in Wales'. Inquiry. 2018. http://senedd.assembly.wales/mgIssueHistoryHome.aspx?IId=21238.

Nelson, Robin. *State of Play: Contemporary "High-End" TV Drama.* Manchester: Manchester University Press, 2007.

Piper, Helen. *The TV Detective.* London: I.B. Tauris, 2015.

Polan, Dana. *The Sopranos.* Durham: Duke University Press, 2009.

Raats, Tim, Tom Evens and Sanne Ruelens. 'Challenges for Sustaining Local Audiovisual Ecosystems: Analysis of Financing and Production of Domestic TV Fiction in Small Media Markets'. *Journal of Popular Television* 4, 1 (2016): 129–147.

Redvall, Eva Novrup. *Writing and Producing Television Drama in Denmark: From The Kingdom to The Killing*. Basingstoke: Palgrave Macmillan, 2013.

Schlesinger, Philip. 'The Creative Economy: Invention of a Global Orthodoxy'. *Enjeux de l'Information et de la Communication* 17, 2 (2016): 187–205.

Stewart, Mark. 'The Myth of Televisual Ubiquity'. *Television & New Media* 17, 8 (2016): 691–705.

Thornham, Sue and Tony Purvis. *Television Drama: Theories and Identities*. Basingstoke: Palgrave, 2005.

Toft Hansen, Kim and Anne Marit Waade. *Locating Nordic Noir: From Beck to The Bridge*. London: Palgrave Macmillan, 2017.

Turnbull, Sue. *The TV Crime Drama*. Edinburgh: Edinburgh University Press, 2014.

Waade, Anne Marit, Eva Novrup Redvall and Pia Majbritt Jensen (eds). *Danish Television Drama: Global Lessons from a Small Nation*. London: Palgrave Macmillan, forthcoming.

Filmography

A Discovery of Witches (Bad Wolf 2018–present).

Call the Midwife (Neal Street Productions/British Broadcasting Corporation 2012–present).

Craith/Hidden (Severn Screen 2018–present).

Derry Girls (Hat Trick Productions 2018–present).

Doctor Who (BBC Wales 2005–present).

Downton Abbey (Carnival Films/ITV Studios 2010–2015).

Fall, The (Artists Studio/BBC Northern Ireland 2013–2016).

Game of Thrones (Home Box Office (HBO)/ Television 360/ Grok! Studio/ Generator Entertainment/Bighead Littlehead 2011–2019).

Happy Valley (Red Production 2014–present).

His Dark Materials (Bad Wolf/ British Broadcasting Corporation/New Line Cinema/Scholastic 2019–present).

Life on Mars (Kudos Film and Television/ British Broadcasting Corporation/ Red Planet Pictures 2006–2007).

Outlander (Tall Ship Productions/Story Mining & Supply Co./Left Bank Pictures/Sony Pictures Television/Soundtrack New York 2014–present).

Peaky Blinders (Tiger Aspect Productions 2013–present).

Sex Education (Eleven 2019–present).

Sherlock (Hartswood Films 2010–present).

Shetland (BBC Scotland 2013–present).

Sopranos, The (Home Box Office/Brillstein Entertainment Partners/The Park Entertainment 1999–2007).

Spooks (Kudos Film and Television 2002–2011).

Vera (ITV Studios 2011–present).

West Wing, The (John Wells Productions/Warner Bros. Television 1999–2006).

Y Gwyll/Hinterland (Fiction Factory 2015–present).

CHAPTER 2

What Makes TV Drama Special?

Abstract This chapter identifies the drivers behind television drama's re-emergence as a highly valued form of media output. It provides critical insight into the prominence of television drama in the strategies of publicly funded broadcasters, commercial broadcasters and policy-makers. In doing so, the chapter challenges some of the assumptions underpinning the 'golden age' discourse that sees the current period as one of innovation and abundance. Instead, it argues that television scholars must bring a more critical perspective to bear on the investment in television drama made by broadcasters and policy-makers. The chapter advances scholarship on TV fiction by giving greater precision to the ways in which drama matters in economic, public and political terms and by critically interrogating questions of value.

Keywords Branding · Golden age · Public service broadcasting · Policy · Subscription video on demand (SVoD) · Value

DRAMA'S MYTHICAL 'GOLDEN AGE'

Open the pages of any British media publication and you are likely to come across articles attesting to a new 'golden age' of drama on the small screen. Explaining his move into British television, the bestselling US crime novelist, Harlan Coben, pronounced:

We're living in the golden age of television. Not only all the great British shows - I knew Tom Cullen from *Downton Abbey*, for example - but also American series like *Breaking Bad*, *True Detective*, *Homeland*, *Dexter*, *Game of Thrones* and *The Walking Dead*. TV's a great medium to tell stories with wide, novel-like scope. You can really let characters breath [*sic*]. (Coben cited in Hogan 2016)

In his article 'TV drama: Britain's Got Talent', TV critic Gerard Gilbert argued that 'British audiences have long been in thrall to US drama series. But the BFI's celebration of home-grown television shows that we too have been enjoying a golden age' (Gilbert 2010). Similarly, when the BBC's former controller of drama commissioning, Ben Stephenson, picked up a Royal Television Society (RTS) Judges' Award in 2015 he was 'praised by the panel for helping lead British drama into what many are calling a new golden age' (Gill 2015).

What do critics and industry professionals mean when they speak of a golden age of TV drama? Frequently they use the term as a historical anchor, rooting contemporary drama in an earlier history of television production—a proposed first golden age of drama that, in the UK, is associated with Sydney Newman, creator of ITV's landmark series *Armchair Theatre* (1956–1974) and, in his role as Head of Drama at the BBC, *The Wednesday Play* (1964–1970). Arguably, this reference to an earlier, lionised period is a way of canonising not only individual writers, plays and series, but also television drama itself; to be in a second golden age implies that television drama has a lineage and a succession of triumphs which contemporary productions might follow.

Further, invoking a second golden age has resonance because it captures a sense of the excitement and distinction associated with TV drama among producers, commissioners and audiences alike. Writing about the first golden age, Shaun Sutton (2014, 40; orig. 2000) notes:

In the immediate postwar years, television drama had been amiably looked down on as a poor relation of the theatre, or a cheap way of making bad films. Now it was establishing itself as a separate art, to be taken seriously, rather than to be visited when nothing better was offering.

Today, television drama is increasingly regarded as a place in which film actors and directors actively *want* to work rather than being a second-class form in which they may *have to* seek work. The acclaimed US film-maker Steven Soderbergh, for example, noted at the 2013 Cannes film festival that 'in terms of cultural real estate ... TV has really taken control of the conversation that used to be the reserve of movies. It's sort of a second golden age of television, which is great for the viewers. If you like your stories to go narrow and deep, TV is exciting' (Soderbergh cited in Lawson 2013).

However, a limitation of the second golden age discourse is that it implies that drama disappeared from television screens and, of course, this was never the case. Television drama has remained a hugely popular staple of the schedules, from one-off 'event television' to returning series. In the UK continuous running dramas, including soap operas, are transmitted in primetime schedules and consistently appear in the Broadcasters Audience Research Board (BARB) weekly lists of most watched television programmes. As we will examine in this chapter, drama is also at the centre of the competitive strategies of broadcasters, screen agencies and some independent producers. Therefore, while we are sceptical of the specific *analytic* value of the concept of a 'golden age', we nonetheless believe that contemporary television drama is enjoying renewed visibility and significance.

The emphasis on television drama is, at least in part, a turn away from other genres that enjoyed a significant period of pre-eminence at the end of the twentieth century. In the 1990s other genres were perceived to overtake drama in terms of innovation, revenue and competition. During this era popular factual entertainment came to the fore, displacing drama and documentary from primetime slots in the evening schedules (see Brunsdon 2003; Moseley 2000). Reality television, gameshows and life-style formats came to be regarded as television's innovators, a view often perpetuated by television scholars as '[i]t was assumed that soap opera was no longer the prism through which television could be understood as a medium' and that instead 'it was *Big Brother* (2000–2018) that became the subject of special issues and major books' (Geraghty 2010, 89). The upsurge in factual entertainment was driven by growing global markets within which relatively cheap formats could be localised to suit different national contexts (see Moran 2009; Esser 2016). Moreover, this decade saw the increased prominence of live sports on television, fuelled by highly competitive bidding wars between satellite, commercial and public service broadcasters, especially for lucrative football rights in the UK.

With viewing figures across many UK channels falling, the early 2000s saw a new wave of imported American drama. Whereas earlier imports such as *Dallas* (1978–1991) and *Dynasty* (1981–1989) had been critically derided despite being hugely popular with audiences, series such as *The Sopranos* (1999–2007), *The West Wing* (1999–2006) and *Six Feet Under* (2001–2005) gained rave reviews and were lauded as superior examples of genuine quality and innovation. This came to be termed in the scholarship as 'quality TV' (see Jancovich and Lyons 2003; McCabe and Akass 2007). For Channel 4, where most of these imports found a home, drama operated as a significant brand marker that announced the channel's riskier creative approach. British television fiction seemed to have been outshone by other genres and by these niche imports. However, as this chapter demonstrates, the value of drama for different stakeholders has now become prominent as competition for audiences and advertising revenue intensifies and the value of niche audiences and discerning subscribers has grown.

The Economic Value of TV Drama

Drama is a hugely popular form with an ability to attract considerable audiences in both domestic and international markets. It has the potential to deliver significant economic return through delivering high audience ratings, retaining the loyalty of subscribers, and securing attractive advertising and licencing opportunities. However, drama is also one of the most expensive and complex television forms to produce and as such it is at a premium. Even experienced producers and commissioners cannot know for sure what an audience will enjoy or what will prove popular. The riskiness, coupled with exceptionally high cost, means that typically screen producers 'do not place all their eggs in one basket, but rely on a slate of investments, carefully managing licensed sales and screenings over time' (Turnbull and McCutcheon 2017, 58). Indeed, drama content is now at the core of a range of 'transmedia franchises' which draw revenue from DVD sales, licencing deals and product extensions such as mobile games. Therefore, making television drama is potentially lucrative but it is a highly risky business.

One of the ways to offset some of the risks of its production is through owning the rights to the content. There is a considerable strategic value for broadcasters and independent producers in owning the rights to a successful series whether that be as an original commission or in securing the exclusive rights for a specific platform or territory. For example, in 2018 Netflix paid WarnerMedia around $100 million (£76m) to keep the rights for 2019 for the show *Friends* (1994–2004), at the time the most streamed show in the UK (Ofcom 2018a). Why would Netflix pay this amount? One of the principal ways in which television drama is significant for broadcasters and content providers is as a differentiator in a crowded marketplace. In the era of channel and platform abundance, drama is a marker of distinction.

Part of television drama's renewed prominence lies in the proliferation of digital channels and the resulting need to fill services with content. The development of niche channels, including public service ones, has been central to the segmenting and ever more precise targeting of audiences. This is exemplified in the UK by BBC Four, which developed a strategic focus on imported high-end European drama, especially crime as one way of distinguishing itself and attracting discerning older viewers (Mazdon 2012; McCabe 2016). The range of niche channels available to British audiences and dedicated to fiction on Freeview (including Drama, ITV3, 5USA, Pick, and CBS Drama) illustrates the strategic targeting of content.[1] The schedules of many of these are dominated by repeats as they leverage the enduring shelf-life of drama. On an international scale, this strategic push to create lucrative content libraries is exemplified by Disney's 2018 purchase of the catalogue of Fox, one of the most prolific content producers in the global television industry. The deal included rights to drama such as *This Is Us* (2016–present), *Modern Family* (2009–present), *American Horror Story* (2011–present) and *Homeland* (2011–present), illustrating Disney's decisive move into streaming services as a complement to its existing linear services. Having a library of original and popular dramas is vital to the contemporary business model of the television industries.

For a pay-TV satellite provider such as Sky, the drive towards drama is also about retaining subscribers and is a response to competition from SVoD services and telecommunications firms. Telecommunications companies have aggressively moved into TV distribution (such as BT in the UK and Telefónica's Movistar+ in Spain). While primarily focussing on

---

[1] Launched in 2002, Freeview is the most watched digital TV service in the UK—around 19 million homes use the service (Freeview 2019). It operates as a joint venture between the BBC, ITV, Channel 4, Sky and transmitter operator Arqiva. As of 2018, more than 60 free-to-air channels and up to 15 HD channels were available on the service.

acquiring sports and movie rights television drama helps Sky to distinguish and elevate its own offering and retain its appeal to monthly subscribers. Sky's strategy has been to use its drama budget to secure exclusive rights to blockbuster imported content such as *Westworld* (2016–present) and *Game of Thrones* (2011–2019) from US cable networks such as Showtime and HBO. Some of these dramas will have already proved popular with UK audiences, having been previously available on free-to-air channels; as exemplified by *Mad Men* (2007–2015), which in the UK aired initially on BBC Four but which was bought by Sky in 2010. This pattern sees publicly funded broadcasters take on the initial work of acquisition and take the risk with a new series before Sky outbids them for later seasons, thereby removing popular series from universal access.

Sky has extended its strategy from importing existing US drama to investing in new commissions, such as *The Tunnel* (2013–2018), an adaptation of the Danish–Swedish crime series *Bron/Broen/The Bridge* (2011–2018). In April 2016, Sky announced six new dramas, stating:

> Sky today announced an impressive roll call of award-winning actors, writers and producers in its most ambitious slate of original productions yet, adding to its growing portfolio of high-quality drama.
>
> Responding to demand from customers for more original drama, the new productions combine with Sky's ground-breaking HBO and Showtime partnerships, to build on its growing reputation as one of the world's best storytellers.

Evidently, Sky sees significant market value in being able to brand itself a world-class 'storyteller' and feels best able to realise these ambitions by co-producing with US cable networks that have an established reputation for high-end TV drama. *Britannia* (2018–present) illustrates this clearly as it is the broadcaster's first co-production with Amazon US, and is transmitted on Sky One in the UK and on Amazon Prime Video in the US.

One of Sky's more recent strategies has been a collaboration with its rival, Netflix. As part of the Sky Q package (Sky's premium subscription service), users can now access content from Netflix.[2] Sky's homepage

---

[2] In 2012 Sky launched its own streaming service, Now TV. In 2017 Now TV was the fastest-growing streaming service in the UK with a subscription base of around 1.4 million UK households, 70% more than in the previous year (Reynolds 2018).

and electronic programme guide (EPG) have been redesigned to incorporate Netflix content and the extension of Sky's drama library is at the forefront of its marketing push to new subscribers. Part of the strategy can be attributed to Sky's stagnating subscriber numbers and a decline in young subscribers (Reynolds 2018), but it also demonstrates how both co-production of content and the distribution of competing content is a striking characteristic of the contemporary television landscape. Sky's investment in original TV drama and its collaboration with Netflix is both a response to viewers' ability to choose and a recognition that original drama production is risky but a powerful commercial asset.

For many broadcasters and platforms, especially the commercial PSBs ITV, Channel 4 and Channel 5, advertising remains their main source of revenue. The advertising market is driven by a range of economic factors, however, television has been more resilient compared to other sectors especially as online businesses like Amazon continue to invest in TV campaigns. Drama's ability to deliver audiences makes it a vital space to place high-profile advertisements and sponsorship. John Lewis' highly anticipated 2018 Christmas advert (The Boy and The Piano) premiered on ITV during the drama *Dark Heart* (2018). And broadcasters are finding new ways to creatively immerse advertising in the viewing experience on both linear and on demand recognising viewers have more control to fast forward through the commercial breaks. Since 2014 'Drama on 4', Channel 4's premium drama strand, has been sponsored by the luxury car manufacturer Lexus. Viewers to linear and on demand services will see ads for Lexus feature in the idents and programme breaks of critically acclaimed shows such as *Homeland* (2011–present), *Fargo* (2014–present) and *The Good Wife* (2009–2016) in this way strategically matching an up-market and wealthy audience (Thinkbox 2016) with the advertiser and offering a return to both.

Finally, demand for drama in the contemporary television ecology is being driven by the expansion and proliferation of online platforms. Original drama is at a premium because it enhances the value proposition of subscription services; distinctive content helps secure viewers' willingness to subscribe. Drama accounts for 70% of Subscription Video on Demand (SVoD) TV programme viewing (Ofcom 2018a, 50). This has had the effect of challenging existing forms of audience measurement, forcing broadcasters, regulators, and services such as Nielsen in the US (Strangelove 2015) and BARB in the UK to reconceptualise their audience and strive for new rating methods that better reflect the growing popularity of online viewing. 'Binge-viewing' as a form of television consumption has become increasingly common, especially among younger age groups who are less wedded to traditional linear schedules. The 2017 Ofcom's Communications Market Report, for example, noted that 53% of teenagers in the UK engage in binge-viewing weekly (Ofcom 2018b, 21). However, we should be wary of conceiving of binge-viewing as normative. Rather, it is a consumption practice produced through a new online distribution strategy in which high-end drama and other select content is released with all episodes in a season made available simultaneously. This is a deliberate tactic of providers such as Netflix to retain audiences, but increasingly public broadcasters have followed suit. For example, the BBC has moved to a 'box set' offering on its iPlayer service and experimenting in releasing the entire series of *Killing Eve* (Sid Gentle Films, 2018–present) as a box set whilst also transmitting it through the established weekly schedule. Netflix's characteristic 'push' of the next drama episode almost before the viewer can draw breath is a commercial tactic to retain viewers, the online corollary of techniques such as 'hammocking' in the traditional linear model of television. The episodic nature of drama series is thus a means by which audiences can be hooked and limits the potential for them to click away. This offers real monetary value in an era of abundance, choice and fragmentation.

CULTURAL VALUE AND THE PUBLIC GOOD

In the UK, public service broadcasters BBC, ITV, Channel 4, Channel 5 and S4C remain the primary source of television drama production—a stark fact that counters headlines related to television's 'revolution'.[3] While Netflix and Amazon invest heavily in original content, currently little is produced in the UK (Ofcom 2018a, 49). In 2017 the total spend on first-run, UK-originated drama by the five main PSB channels and BBC portfolio channels was £307m (Ofcom 2018a, 45).[4] These sums

---

[3]This book adopts Ofcom's definition of PSB as the BBC, Channel 4, the Channel 3 Licensees (ITV and STV), Channel 5 and S4C, the Welsh-language channel. All BBC services are PSB, but only the main channels of the other broadcasters have public service obligations.

[4]These figures do not take into consideration contributions to the cost of production from third parties, such as overseas broadcasters and independent production companies, under co-production arrangements.

are considerable, but they also show a decline in funding to UK television drama production (a decline of 7% from 2016 (ibid))—a truth that cuts against the golden age discourse.

Investment in original drama by public service broadcasters such as the BBC, ITV and, more recently, Channel 4, S4C and latterly Channel 5, has been partially in response to accusations of producing overly commercial, cheap content that cannot easily be distinguished from the offerings of commercial broadcasters. As Bennett argues, the ideal of independence has 'seen the British television industry marked by tension and compromise between the ideal of political independence, on the one hand, and the free market and economic and entrepreneurial independence on the other' (2015, 71). So, for example, Channel 5 has replaced the costly reality format Big Brother with original drama commissions such as Irish acquisition *Blood* (2018–present) and *15 Days* (2019–present) which is based on S4C's original Welsh-language drama *35 Diwrnod* (2014–present). Channel 5's Director of Programmes, Ben Frow, explained how 'home grown drama is the missing ingredient from Channel 5s schedules' (Munn 2018) demonstrating that even smaller commercial PSBs no longer feel able to ignore drama. Public service broadcasters thus stand to gain ratings, prestige, higher levels of appreciation and overall support when delivering dramas that are popular and/or critically acclaimed. ITV's 'Where Drama Lives' branding campaign is, as Garner (2016) demonstrates, a good example of how a commercial public service broadcaster catering to a mainstream audience on a general channel can use popular drama as a way of emphasising its quality provision and its heritage as a provider of watchable, returning series. Thus, ITV (2018) explain how their soaps *Coronation Street* (1960–present) and *Emmerdale* (1972–present) have been 'entertaining the nation for decades and are at the heart of the national conversation on a daily basis' while also providing a 'solid inheritance for our 9 pm dramas'.

Drama's range and imaginative capacity to represent social change help distinguish broadcasters' offering to the public. Receiving an Outstanding Contribution to Writing Award, Heidi Thomas (*Call the Midwife* 2012) put it succinctly, 'People need stories... people need to be transported... people need to feel that their lives matter' (Writers' Guild 2019). This emphasis on the needs, pleasures and interpretative capabilities of television drama audiences is too often eclipsed by economically driven analyses of production. As Forrest and Johnson (2017) argue, the narrative conjunction of quality with financial input into drama production conceals the inherently classed nature of many scholarly evaluations of television drama and underplays a wider conception of the public good.

For PSBs, drama is a vital resource in securing the public and political support they need to be sustainable. The cultural value of drama is especially significant to the BBC (and latterly S4C) given that its funding system—the licence fee paid by all owners of television sets and users of its online catch-up service—is frequently the subject of debate in the UK press, particularly during periods when its Charter is up for renewal.[5] The endurance of this funding model sets the UK apart from many European countries which have done away with licence fees. This universal licence fee model is often cited by critics as anachronistic in an age where households frequently purchase customised subscriptions to other satellite, cable and SVoD providers. In other European countries such as Denmark, the licence fee model has been replaced by a digital media tax (see McElroy et al. 2018). In Switzerland, a referendum on the licence fee was defeated with 71% of the population voting against its abolition with supporters arguing that 'it is essential to a small country [..] to have a national broadcaster which reflects its cultural and linguistic diversity' (BBC 2018a). Moreover, the continuation of the licence fee in the UK has meant that the BBC has escaped the demands of advertisers and has instilled in British viewers an expectation of a plural, diverse service premised on a range of original UK-made productions across all genres and catering to a broad range of tastes. Drama, therefore, can garner significant cultural and political value for PSBs when it proves popular with audiences and licence-fee payers, who are then more likely to see value in the broadcasters' continued existence. As Ben Stephenson, former Controller of BBC Drama, puts it:

> Drama gets big ratings, which is an important part of what we do. It has the talkability factor. The sense of drama being at the heart of the BBC alongside news is absolutely key. It defines us and makes us distinctive. (Szalai interview with Stephenson 2014)

[5] The way the BBC is governed and funded is set out by Royal Charter and this forms the constitutional basis for its operation. The BBC's new Charter commenced on 1 January 2017 and was preceded by a period of negotiation with the government, specifically the Department for Digital, Culture, Media & Sport (DCMS).

In a climate where UK press and politicians, especially those on the right of the political spectrum, are voluble in their criticisms of PSBs, ratings successes provide a valuable defence of both the distinctive contribution of PSBs and, in the case of the BBC, the licence fee.

Indeed, ratings have evolved to become a significant ideological instrument in public service broadcasting's claims to legitimacy. Ratings inhabit the public domain not merely as statistical measurements, but as rhetorical tools deployed by stakeholders—ranging from schedulers to producers to channel controllers—in order to legitimise their own service. As Bourdon and Méadel (2014, 6) argue, 'these professional indicators not only determine the price of a service' but they are 'also a poll (reflecting public opinion) and a vote (they confer legitimacy on certain cultural content, certain personalities—TV hosts, journalists— and certain institutions—TV channels'. Drama series, especially crime, deliver ratings, audience appreciation and social media chatter. For example, in Autumn 2018 *Bodyguard* was the most watched BBC drama since 2008 drawing an average 10.4 million viewers with the series finale driving the iPlayer's biggest day ever with over 12.6m requests (BBC 2018b). Drama is an essential asset for PSBs emphasising the unique power of their content to cement valuable relationships with audiences, advertisers and politicians.

This kind of high-profile asset becomes even more valuable with the entry of new SVoD services such as Amazon Prime, Hulu, Apple and Netflix into the television marketplace and their focus on commissioning original drama with high production values. These businesses are enormously well-resourced, with *The Economist* (2018) reporting that Netflix will spend $12bn–13bn (approx. £9.5bn) on content in 2018, $3bn–4bn (approx. £3bn) more than the previous year. For context, that *extra* spending alone would be enough to pay for all of the BBC's content in every genre (ibid). Many SVoD providers are able to invest huge sums in both acquisitions and original content, while their business model allows them to use what would often be considered niche dramas to drive increased subscriptions. Netflix's historical drama, *The Crown* (2016–present), is one of the most expensive television series ever made, with a budget of around £100 million, signalling the company's move into content previously dominated by national broadcasters and of particular appeal to relatively older, richer subscribers. As the BBC's then Director of Television Danny Cohen admitted, the corporation 'couldn't compete with the amount of money that Netflix were prepared to pay' for 'a classic BBC subject' (Cohen cited in Martinson 2016).

The iPlayer—created in 2007 and branded by the BBC as 'making the unmissable, unmissable'—features drama prominently using the platform to support content diversification, talent development and programme experimentation (Grainge and Johnson 2018, 38). While there are obstacles to the realisation of full public value online (see Ramsey 2013), the BBC regards iPlayer as drawing 'hard to reach' audiences to these services, especially young people, and ensures that drama has enhanced value beyond the time of its transmission on linear services. In 2018 BBC and ITV announced a new joint online service, Britbox, to offer British-made drama to subscribers in the UK and internationally. The service will include both new and classic series, incentivising the broadcasters to retain the rights for popular content; for instance, at the time of writing, *Peaky Blinders* (BBC) and *Victoria* (ITV) were licensed to Netflix. Such commercial strategies demonstrate the underlying global collaboration between providers, including larger national public service broadcasters like the BBC which are adopting an array of commercially driven strategies. These strategies are legitimised on the basis firstly of needing to compete with global firms like Netflix and, secondly, on the basis that this will generate revenue to help fund the domestic service: 'Through its commercial activities the BBC seeks to deliver additional value for licence fee payers by providing extra funding for BBC programmes, by contributing to the BBC's Public Purposes, and by promoting the BBC brand around the world' (Public Accounts Committee 2018, summary). However, success is far from guaranteed and such entries into the market for international distribution risk detracting from the specific domestic purposes of a public service broadcaster.

THE POLITICAL VALUE OF TV DRAMA

The political value of television drama production to regional and national policy-makers has greatly increased in recent years. This is partly a result of the rise of the creative industries on politicians' agendas both in the UK and beyond (see Schlesinger 2016). In a post-industrial era, where competition has driven down global production costs, the value of creating high-quality, exportable Intellectual Property (IP) like TV content, has grown exponentially. Moreover, the distinctive value of skilled labour in producing such IP has become integral to industrial and economic policies geared towards stimulating a highly skilled growth industry. Therefore, for policy-makers, television drama production is at the nexus of economic development, cultural representation, place or nation branding, improvements in local infrastructure and local job markets. Television drama and the structures of its production are seen as potentially transformative, changing the economic fortunes of a place and enhancing its visibility globally.

For policy-makers and politicians, the value of television drama lies partly in its potential to deliver substantial economic returns. It has become an integral element in the export strategy of UK creative industries. For instance, PACT's 2014/2015 'UK Television Exports' survey notes that 'drama was a key driver of British export success with respondents reporting that this form, although relatively small in size, sold to the greatest number of territories' (2015, 3).[6] There is also clear political value to be gained from the visibility of British television internationally; drama as a prestige form stands out in this context. For example, in his foreword to the 2015/2016 PACT 'UK Television Exports' report, Mark Garnier, then Parliamentary Under Secretary of State at the Department for International Trade (DIT), noted:

> From *The Night Manager* to *Downton Abbey*, UK TV exports continue to go from strength to strength. The UK is a world leader in the sales of TV content globally and revenues continue to rise [...] UK programmes are some of the most recognisable and eagerly anticipated in the world. British innovation and creativity, allied with high production values and the ownership of Intellectual Property that can be exploited globally, are considered among the greatest assets of the UK television sector. (PACT 2017, 2)

Television drama is frequently lauded by politicians in their discourse on creative industries and is seen by them as one of the UK's great cultural and trade assets. This explains why governments are prepared simultaneously to invest public money in making television programmes ostensibly for viewers beyond their own shores, while at the same point, making substantial funding cuts to PSBs.

---

[6] PACT is the UK trade association representing the commercial interests of independent television, film, digital, children's and animation media companies. For more information see www.pact.co.uk.

Policy-makers deploy several instruments to support the television sector including legislative changes and fiscal levers. For instance, the Broadcasting Act (1990) created the conditions that aided the growth of independent television producers by requiring the BBC and ITV to source programme content from external providers and subject to minimum quotas.[7] This was followed over a decade later by another transformative piece of policy. Until 2003, UK broadcasters operated a 'cost plus system'. This meant that while they funded the cost of programme production, they crucially retained most rights for secondary domestic and overseas sales. Following effective lobbying of policy-makers by PACT as part of the negotiations of the 2003 Communications Act, UK independent production companies were granted beneficial 'terms of trade' meaning that today they retain and can profit from back-end rights to their own productions (Lee 2018; Steemers 2016). Owning the rights to content is a major pillar in the economic logic of British television production today. Both these political interventions helped foster growth in the independent sector, a component of the UK's television market that we return to in the next chapter.

One of the other prominent examples of policy intervention comes in the form of tax breaks. For scripted TV projects with a core expenditure of at least £1 million per broadcast hour—in effect, high-end drama—this is in the form of a rebate of up to 25% of qualifying UK expenditure by the TV production company.[8] Television programmes must either pass the cultural test administered by the BFI or qualify as a co-production through approved co-production treaties with other countries in order to gain British certification. This fiscal lever, one extended from film policy, is used to attract and retain all elements of production from on-location shooting to pre- and post-production activities. As Magor and Schlesinger outline, the perceived benefits of this policy are threefold:

---

[7] Channel 4, Channel 5 and S4C were established as publisher-broadcasters meaning that they have never been in-house producers of content.

[8] Tax-related investment schemes vary from country to country, but broadly fall into two general categories: direct incentives, such as wage credits, sales tax rebates and reductions or waivers of capital tax, and indirect incentives, which are designed to promote private investments, such as accelerated or preferential depreciation allowances (Morawetz et al. 2007, 430).

For HM Treasury, this is intended first to encourage the production of films that might otherwise not be made, second to promote the 'sustainability' of British film production, and third to maintain a 'critical mass' in the UK's infrastructure for creative and technical skills. (Magor and Schlesinger 2009, 316)

In 2016–2017 there were 45 television programmes completed in the UK in which the production company claimed High-end Television Tax Relief, with UK expenditure of £480 million (HMRC 2017). Since the relief was introduced in 2013, 205 programmes have received funding, supporting £1.5 billion of UK expenditure (ibid.).

The UK is not the only country using fiscal tools to win investment; this in turn makes for a highly competitive environment as there is substantial global competition between regions and nations keen to attract inward investment and build substantial indigenous productions. Television drama production is increasingly driven by the search for financial capital (Morawetz et al. 2007) and tax incentives can drive co-productions (Baltruschat 2010). As one interviewee in our own research concluded:

[T]he way projects are developed is broadcasters and production companies find out what they want to do and then, only after that when the whole thing is clear and packaged, do you start shopping around for the best offers of location, talent, financing and so on in various regions. Even Film i Väst, the Swedish success story, I would say is definitely a commercial success but it's not a regional success to be honest. So, I think we have to look at it in terms of how commodified regional input has become on a European scale because of coproduction markets and so on. (Interview with Danish producer and film consultant, 2016)

The production history of Amazon's first original UK drama *The Collection* (2016) illustrates this mobility and the ways production decisions are driven by capital. The series is set in post-war Paris but was filmed in Wales. Originally the production was due to be filmed in the north of England on the back of an incentive package offered by Screen Yorkshire, the regional screen agency tasked with developing production in the region. The production relocated to Wales following a reduction in the funding available to the production in Yorkshire, along with concerns about the availability of busy local crew. The collapse in scheduled production of the Hollywood remake of the film

The Crow in Wales at the same time meant that Wales was able to attract *The Collection* to its studios along with the support of the Welsh Government's Media Investment Budget. Increasingly, high-end television drama production relies on exploiting this competitive, mobile global infrastructure; it is integral to the rising production values of what we see on screen and to the growth of international co-production as a means of delivering new content to broadcasters and SVoD services.

Television drama production is significant for policy-makers hoping to attract, retain and foster a sustainable production ecology as a direct economic response to post-industrial decline. The television drama industry's global commercial growth is thus built on policies driving publicly funded investment even as cuts are being made to PSBs. Government fiscal levers are subject to some regulation, for example via European rules on state aid, which may alter for the UK if it leaves the European Union. However, as Ramsey et al. (2019) argue, there is an under-developed capability for holding governments to account for these complex investments. As scholars we believe it is vital to test the philosophical underpinnings for using public money in an age of austerity to support global commercial companies. The international visibility and prestige enjoyed by this form, together with the diverse range of skills necessary for its production, makes drama an appealing public investment for politicians. However, for policy-makers the challenge is not only to secure investment from individual productions, but also to sustain the highly-skilled, but highly deregulated, freelance workforce that make these programmes. Without extracting substantial public benefits, the investment of public money in global television drama production seems like a misadventure that does not do justice to the full value of drama to the public good of the UK and its constituent regions and nations.

REFERENCES

Baltruschat, Doris. *Global Media Ecologies: Networked Production in Film and Television*. London: Routledge, 2010.
BBC (a). 'Switzerland TV Licence: Voters Reject Plan to Scrap Fee'. BBC News, 4 March 2018. Accessed 28 March 2019. https://www.bbc.co.uk/news/world-europe-43278646.
BBC (b). 'Bodyguard Most Watched BBC Drama Since 2008'. BBC News, 25 September 2018. Accessed 13 October 2018. https://www.bbc.co.uk/news/entertainment-arts-45622655.

Bennett, James. 'From Independence to Independents, Public Service to Profit: British TV and the Impossibility of Independence'. In *Media Independence: Working with Freedom or Working for Free?* edited by James Bennett and Nikki Strange, 71–93. London: Routledge, 2015.

Bourdon, Jérôme and Cecile Méadel (eds). *Television Audiences Across the World: Deconstructing the Ratings Machine.* London: Palgrave Macmillan, 2014.

Brunsdon, Charlotte. 'Lifestyling Britain: The 8–9 Slot on British Television'. *International Journal of Cultural Studies* 6, 1 (2003): 5–23.

Economist. 'Hollywood Ending: Can Netflix Please Investors and Still Avoid the Techlash'. 28 June 2018. Accessed 20 August 2018. https://www.economist.com/leaders/2018/06/28/can-netflix-please-investors-and-still-avoid-the-techlash.

Esser, Andrea. 'The Format Age: Television's Entertainment Revolution'. *Popular Communication* 14, 4 (2016): 243–246.

Forrest, David and Beth Johnson (eds). *Social Class and Television Drama in Contemporary Britain.* London: Palgrave Macmillan, 2017.

Freeview. 'About Us'. Accessed 19 March 2019 https://www.freeview.co.uk/about-us#2od5Prt82ZrutO2Z.97.

Garner, Ross. 'Crime Drama and Channel Branding: ITV and Broadchurch'. In *Contemporary British Television Crime Drama: Cops on the Box,* edited by Ruth McElroy, 139–153. London: Routledge, 2016.

Geraghty, Christine. 'Exhausted and Exhausting: Television Studies and British Soap Opera'. *Critical Studies in Television* 5, 1 (2010): 82–96.

Gilbert, Gerard. 'TV Drama: Britain's Got Talent'. *The Independent,* 5 May 2010. Accessed 8 August 2018. https://www.independent.co.uk/arts-entertainment/tv/features/tv-drama-britains-got-talent-1962320.html.

Gill, James. 'Drama Boss Ben Stephenson Labels Criticism of the BBC "Effing Nonsense"'. *Radio Times,* 18 March 2015. Accessed 20 August 2018. https://www.radiotimes.com/news/2015-03-18/drama-boss-ben-stephenson-labels-criticism-of-the-bbc-effing-nonsense/.

Grainge, Paul and Catherine Johnson. 'From Catch-Up TV to Online TV: Digital Broadcasting and the Case of BBC iPlayer'. *Screen* 59, 1 (2018): 21–40.

HMRC. 'Creative Industries Statistics July 2017'. 20 July 2017. Accessed 20 August 2018. https://www.gov.uk/government/statistics/creative-industries-statistics-july-2017.

Hogan, Michael. 'Harlan Coben: "We're in the Golden Age of Television"'. *The Telegraph,* 14 April 2016. Accessed 8 August 2018. https://www.telegraph.co.uk/tv/2016/04/14/harlan-coben-were-in-the-golden-age-of-television/.

ITV. 'Commissioning: Drama'. Accessed 8 July 2018. http://www.itv.com/commissioning/drama.

Jancovich, Mark and James Lyons. *Quality Popular Television: Cult TV, the Industry and Fans*. London: British Film Institute, 2003.

Lawson, Mark. 'Are We Really in a "Second Golden Age for Television"?'. *The Guardian*, 23 May 2013. Accessed 20 August 2018. https://www.theguardian.com/tv-and-radio/tvandradioblog/2013/may/23/second-golden-age-television-soderbergh.

Lee, David. *Independent Television Production in the UK: From Cottage Industry to Big Business*. Cham, Switzerland: Palgrave Macmillan, 2018.

Magor, Maggie and Philip Schlesinger. '"For This Relief Much Thanks.' Taxation, Film Policy and the UK Government'. *Screen* 50, 3 (2009): 299–317.

Martinson, Jane. 'Netflix's Glittering Crown Could Leave BBC Looking a Little Dull'. *The Guardian*, 31 October 2016. Accessed 18 June 2018. https://www.theguardian.com/media/2016/oct/31/netflix-glittering-crown-bbc-dull-launch-tv.

Mazdon, Lucy. 'Spiral on BBC4: Putting Quality First?' *Critical Studies in Television* 7, 2 (2012): 112–119.

McCabe, Janet. 'Wallander at the BBC: Trading Fiction, Producing Culture and UK Public Service Broadcasting in the Contemporary Age'. In *New Patterns in Global Television Formats*, edited by Karina Aveyard, Pia Majbritt Jensen and Albert Moran, 171–186. Bristol: Intellect Books, 2016.

McCabe, Janet and Kim Akass (eds). *Quality TV: Contemporary American Television and Beyond*. London: I.B. Tauris, 2007.

McElroy, Ruth, Caitriona Noonan and Jakob Isak Nielsen 'Small Is Beautiful? The Salience of Scale and Power to Three European Cultures of TV Production'. *Critical Studies in Television* 13, 2 (2018): 169–187.

Moran, Albert. *New Flows in Global TV*. Bristol: Intellect, 2009.

Morawetz, Norbert, Jane Hardy, Colin Haslam and Keith Randle. Finance, Policy and Industrial Dynamics: The Rise of Co-productions in the Film Industry. *Industry and Innovation* 14, 4 (2007): 421–443.

Moseley, Rachel. 'Makeover Takeover on British Television'. *Screen* 41, 3 (2000): 299–314.

Munn, Patrick 'Channel 5 Continues Drama Push'. TV Wise, 19 September 2018. Accessed 24 March 2019. https://www.tvwise.co.uk/2018/09/channel-5-continues-drama-push-with-clink-15-days-feature-length-murder-mystery/.

Ofcom (a). 'Media Nations: UK 2018'. 18 July 2018. Accessed 22 August 2018. https://www.ofcom.org.uk/research-and-data/tv-radio-and-on-demand/media-nations.

Ofcom (b). 'Communications Market Report 2017'. 17 August 2018. Accessed 21 August 2018. https://www.ofcom.org.uk/research-and-data/multi-sector-research/cmr/cmr-2017.

PACT. 'UK Television Exports 2014–2015'. 1 October 2015. Accessed 24 August 2018. http://www.pact.co.uk/news-detail.html?id=africa-buys-up-british-tv-programmes.

PACT. 'UK Television Exports 2015–2016'. 3 February 2017. Accessed 24 August 2018. http://www.pact.co.uk/news-detail.html?id=impressive-growth-in-uk-television-exports-up-10-to-1-326m.

Public Accounts Committee. 'BBC Commercial Activities'. HC June 2018, Para 23. https://publications.parliament.uk/pa/cm201719/cmselect/cmpubacc/670/67002.htm.

Ramsey, Phil. 'The Search for a Civic Commons Online: An Assessment of Existing BBC Online Policy'. *Media, Culture and Society* 35, 7 (2013): 864–879.

Ramsey, Phil, Steve Baker and Robert Porter. 'Screen Production "on the Biggest Set in the World": Northern Ireland Screen and the Case of *Game of Thrones*'. *Media, Culture and Society*, 2019. https://doi.org/10.1177/0163443719831597.

Reynolds, Matt. 'Adding Netflix Won't Save Sky, But That's Not the Point of the Deal'. *Wired*, 2 March 2018. Accessed 8 November 2018. https://www.wired.co.uk/article/netflix-sky-streaming-deal-sky-q-disney-fox-comcast.

Schlesinger, Philip. 'The Creative Economy: Invention of a Global Orthodoxy'. *Enjeux de l'Information et de la Communication* 17, 2 (2016): 187–205.

Sutton, Shaun. 'Sydney Newman and the "Golden Age"'. In *British Television Drama: Past, Present and Future*, edited by Bignell, Jonathan and Stephen Lacey, 40–44. 2nd edition. Basingstoke: Palgrave Macmillan, 2014.

Steemers, Jeanette. 'International Sales of UK Television Content: Change and Continuity in "the Space in Between" Production and Consumption'. *Television and New Media* 17, 8 (2016): 734–753.

Strangelove, Michael. *Post-TV: Piracy, Cord-Cutting and the Future of Television*. Toronto: University of Toronto Press, 2015.

Szalai, Georg. 'BBC Drama Chief Talks Global Hits and Impact, U.S. Partners, Need for Ambitious Shows'. *The Hollywood Reporter*, 19 November 2014. Accessed 21 August 2018. https://www.hollywoodreporter.com/news/bbc-drama-chief-talks-global-750298.

Thinkbox. 'Lexus Changes Gear with Drama on 4'. 10 May 2016. Accessed 17 March 2019. https://www.thinkbox.tv/Case-studies/Lexus.

Turnbull, Sue and Marion McCutcheon. 'Investigating Miss Fisher: The Value of a Television Crime Drama'. *Media International Australia* 164, 1 (2017): 56–70.

Writers' Guild. 'Award Winners 2019'. 14 January 2019. Accessed 24 March 2019 https://writersguild.org.uk/writers-guild-award-winners-2019/.

Filmography

15 Days (Boom 2019–present).

35 Diwrnod (Boom Apollo 2014–present).

American Horror Story (20th Century Fox Television 2011–present).

Armchair Theatre (ABC Weekend Television 1956, Thames Television 1969–1974).

Wednesday Play, The (British Broadcasting Company 1964–1970).

Big Brother (Bazal, Brighter Pictures, Channel 4 Television Corporation 2000–2018).

Blood (Company Pictures 2018–present).

Bodyguard (World Productions 2018).

Britannia (Amazon Studios, Film United, Neal Street Productions, Sky, Vertigo Films 2018–present).

Bron/Broen/The Bridge (Filmlance International AB, Nimbus Film Productions 2011–2018).

Collection, The (Lookout Point 2016).

Coronation Street (Granada Television 1960–present).

Crown, The (Left Bank Pictures/Sony Pictures Television Production UK 2016–present).

Dallas (Lorimar Productions/Lorimar Telepictures/Lorimar Television 1978–1991).

Dark Heart (ITV Studios 2018).

Downton Abbey (Carnival Films/ITV Studios 2010–2015).

Dynasty (Aaron Spelling Productions 1981–1989).

Emmerdale (Yorkshire Television (YTV) 1972–present).

Fargo (MGM Television/FX Productions/26Keys Productions 2014–present).

Friends (Warner Bros.Television/Bright/Kauffman/Crane Productions 1994–2004).

Game of Thrones (Home Box Office (HBO)/ Television 360/ Grok! Studio/ Generator Entertainment/Bighead Littlehead 2011–2019).

Good Wife, The (Scott Free Productions/ King Size Productions/Small Wishes/ CBS Productions/CBS Television Studios 2009–2016).

Homeland (Teakwood Lane Productions/Cherry Pie Productions/Keshet Broadcasting/Fox 21/Showtime Networks 2011–present).

Killing Eve (Sid Gentle Films 2018–).

Mad Men (Lionsgate Television/Weiner Bros. American Movie Classics/ U.R.O.K Productions 2007–2015).

Modern Family (Levitan/Lloyd/20th Century Fox Television/Steven Levitan Productions/Picador Productions 2009–present).

Night Manager, The (BBC/AMC/The Ink Factory/Demarest Films/Character 7/ Producciones Fortaleza AIE 2016).

Peaky Blinders (Tiger Aspect Productions 2013–present).

Six Feet Under (Home Box Office/The Greenblatt Janollari Studio/Actual Size Films/Actual Size Productions 2001–2005).

Sopranos, The (Home Box Office/Brillstein Entertainment Partners/The Park Entertainment 1999–2007).

This Is Us (Rhode Island Ave. Productions/Zaftig Films/20th Century Fox Television 2016–present).

Tunnel, The (Canal+/Kudos Film and Television/Shine/Sky Atlantic 2013–2018).

Victoria (Mammoth Screen/Masterpiece 2016–present).

West Wing, The (John Wells Productions/Warner Bros. Television 1999–2006).

Westworld (Bag Robot/Jerry Weintraub Productions/Kilter Films/Warner Bros. Television 2016–present).

CHAPTER 3

The Ecology of TV Drama Production

Abstract This chapter provides an original analysis of the ecology of contemporary British television drama production. It identifies the vital role played by public service broadcasters in maintaining a plural domestic production industry. We isolate three key elements in the production and distribution of drama. Firstly, the commissioning process itself is interrogated as an occupational practice that centralises power in the hands of commissioners who are often distant from local ecologies of production. Secondly, the role of independent production companies ('indies') and the increasing move towards national and international co-production deals is understood as a direct response to the mobility of television content and the riskiness of its production. Finally, we examine the challenges presented by the rise of subscription video on demand (SVoD) providers, such as Netflix, Amazon Prime, Disney and Apple, to the existing business models, intellectual property rights ownership and broader relationships between PSBs and the UK's indies. We argue that the production practices of contemporary British television drama reveal meaningful tensions between primarily national models of PSB-funded drama production serving plural audiences and export-driven production models in which the unregulated power of major global firms is being consolidated.

Keywords BBC Studios · Commissioning · Co-production ·
Independent production · Public service broadcasting · Rights ·
Subscription video on demand (SVoD)

© The Author(s) 2019
R. McElroy and C. Noonan, *Producing British Television Drama*,
https://doi.org/10.1057/978-1-137-57875-4_3

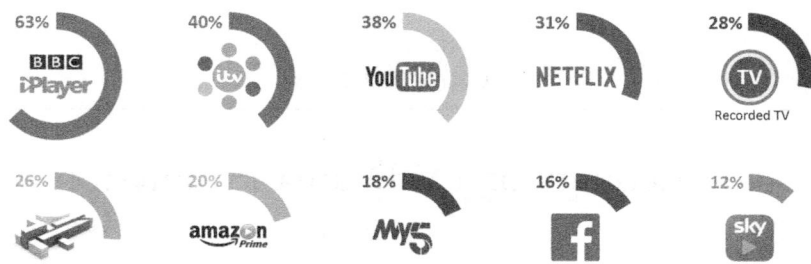

Fig. 3.1 Proportion of adults who use different service for watching TV programmes/films (*Image source* Ofcom 2018b, 13)

While the making of television drama is part of a global production and distribution system, this system has distinct, meaningful national characteristics. In the UK, one of the most fundamental of these characteristics is the central role played by the public service broadcasters (PSBs). Despite considerable audience fragmentation in the digital era, audiences continue to watch and value public service broadcasting. Satisfaction with public service broadcasting overall is in line with recent years, with 75% of viewers claiming to be either very or quite satisfied with the service (Ofcom 2018a, 5), while at the same time public broadcasters have maintained their share of broadcast viewing (ibid.). Half (51%) of all broadcast viewing on the TV is to the main five PSB channels: BBC One, BBC Two, Channel 3 (known as ITV in England and Wales; STV in Scotland, and UTV in Northern Ireland), Channel 4 and Channel 5. Meanwhile, BBC iPlayer is the most popular on-demand/streaming service in the UK among adults (Ofcom 2018b) (Fig. 3.1).

In the absence of PSBs, few UK drama series would get made. Culturally and economically, PSBs play a vital role in commissioning and making some of the UK's most popular continuous series and the kind of high-profile, big-budget returning productions that win audience approval in the UK and internationally. From *Doctor Who* (2005–present) to *Sherlock* (2010–present) and *Downton Abbey* (2010–2015) to *War and Peace* (2016), it is the PSBs who commission most of the drama consumed by UK television audiences and who are the main buyers of original drama content from UK independent production companies ('indies'). In doing so, they are adhering to a regulatory regime that requires most PSBs to produce diverse original content and to support the UK's creative economy. In 2016, the four main terrestrial networks accounted for an estimated 82% of UK primary commission spend within the independent sector (PACT 2017b, 13). This commissioning pipeline supports an entire ecology of independent production companies and freelancers. Paradoxically, this pipeline is also one reason why international firms such as Discovery, Canal+ and Time Warner have increasingly been attracted to acquiring UK indies, alongside access to the local talent base and the rights models secured by the 'terms of trade', which are discussed below.

Unlike many European countries, UK viewers have access to a high number of original, domestic drama series which are available for all to view on the main free-to-air public service broadcasting channels. Access to this range of original drama is largely taken for granted by British viewers who have long enjoyed the privilege of being able to consume quality UK content. However, the reality of the 'golden age', which we critiqued in the previous chapter, is that most broadcasters do not, and indeed cannot, produce a high volume of original drama. As a stark example, in 2015 Ireland's public broadcaster RTÉ transmitted only eight and a half hours of home-produced drama across just two series (Slattery 2016). Despite the narrative of abundance and choice (see Stewart 2016), for many audiences, seeing their own places, and hearing their own stories and languages on screen in dramatic narratives is much more intermittent, a tension we return to in more detail in Chapter 4. Furthermore, while the figures spent on drama and soap operas are high, there has been a significant decrease in both spend and the number of hours of original first-run drama (Ofcom 2018a). This decrease is a tangible consequence of government cuts to the public funding of broadcasters such as the BBC and S4C. The year-on-year fall in TV advertising income (down by 7% in real terms) has been felt most acutely by commercial PSBs (ibid.). In 2017, ITV, the UK's largest commercial PSB, reduced the volume of its first-run UK origination drama output to 132 hours, down from 159 hours in 2016 (Ofcom 2018a). Ofcom warns that 'the risks of structural decline appear to be growing as TV viewing falls and online video advertising encroaches on traditional broadcast TV advertising revenue' (Ofcom 2018a, 5). These declines have therefore increased the significance of international revenues to the commissioning and production process. The rise of co-production as the financial model for producing original drama is a consequence of both governmental and industrial drivers. These drivers include public funding cuts, decreasing advertising revenues, escalating production budgets from digital disruptors, governmental tax incentives, and elevated expectations of high production values from audiences, commissioners and reviewers.

Ofcom's data tempers the 'golden age of drama' discourse that tends to highlight prominent high-budget series and new SVoD platforms as evidence of all being well. More importantly, this data evidences that PSBs enjoy continued public support if not from all politicians. As we illustrate throughout this book, PSBs remain central to the UK's television drama ecology and its long-term sustainability. While they undoubtedly face significant industrial and political challenges, news of their demise is premature.

Innovations in the Supply Chain

It is from within this complex, often contradictory, ecology that UK television drama emerges. Most British drama is commissioned from one of a limited number of suppliers, partly as a way of managing the riskiness of its production, the main sources being in-house production departments and independent production companies.[1]

Historically, most drama emanated from the in-house production units of broadcasters such as the BBC and ITV. Producing drama internally was perceived as a route to ensuring quality and retaining creative control. The marketisation of public service broadcasting culminating in the 1990 Broadcasting Act required 25% of the BBC's production to be outsourced to independents. In 2007, the BBC established its Window of Creative Competition (WoCC) which allowed indies and in-house producers to compete for 25% of programme output with indies proving successful in three-quarters of cases. By 2013, the BBC Trust's Review of the WoCC for television noted that 'independent producers secured 72% and 83% of the available network television hours under the WoCC in 2010–2011 and 2011–2012 respectively' and 'winning a large

---

[1]A third form of production, 'special purpose vehicle' (SPV), may sometimes be created to produce a specific production. This usually occurs where a producer may be involved in several projects and so they might establish individual SPVs, allowing each project to be developed as wholly owned or joint ventures for administrative, accounting and tax purposes. This structure affords some protection against financial liability and is one way in which producers attempt to manage risk inherent within the production process.

proportion of hours in Drama' in the two years under review (2013, 5). Throughout this period, however, 50% of BBC programmes remained in-house at the BBC and today, several BBC dramas are made entirely by parts of the BBC, including BBC Cymru Wales.[2] However, many other high-budget dramas such as the miniseries adaptation of John Le Carré's *The Night Manager* (2016) are made in partnership with several external companies. Increased structural capacity, more risk-taking and the opportunity to own the rights to a successful show in perpetuity are part of the pay-off for broadcasters producing their own content. However, in-house production also involves taking on all the financial and operational risks associated with making content, which can be substantial. Therefore, the trend within the sector is away from traditional forms of in-house production, especially in the case of publicly funded broadcasters under threat from funding cuts and seeking increased efficiency. Instead what has emerged is a strategy of creating new commercial subsidiaries in order to 'wall off' in-house production into a separate entity from the rest of the organisation. This approach has culminated in the creation of BBC Studios and ITV Studios. Arguably, these entities occupy the competitive advantage enjoyed by independent production companies while simultaneously enjoying the considerable assets (including international brand identity) of large-scale PSBs.

In 2017, BBC Studios was launched as a *commercial* production subsidiary of the BBC, akin to BBC Worldwide, with which it merged in 2018 (Public Accounts Committee 2018). The BBC explained the merger in overtly commercial terms as a response to the 'increasingly competitive and global market for production and distribution, this new organisational structure will bring the BBC into line with the rest of the industry, integrating programme production, sales and distribution in a single entity' (BBC 2017).

---

[2] Established in 1964, BBC Cymru Wales is a division of the BBC and the national broadcaster of Wales. It produces a range of content for broadcast in Wales and the rest of the UK in both English and Welsh, operating two TV channels (BBC One Wales, BBC Two Wales) and two radio stations. In recent years, its drama output (e.g. *Casualty* (1986–present), *Doctor Who*, *Torchwood* (2006–2011) and *The Sarah Jane Adventures* (2007–2011) has been particularly successful and, in order to house these productions while expanding their production activities, a state of the art studio complex was built at Roath Lock, Cardiff in 2011 (McElroy and Noonan 2016).

The creation of BBC Studios is one of the most radical changes in the ecology of British television production in recent years.[3] BBC Studios operates in effect as a giant 'indie' and competes as a production company both for BBC commissions and for commissions from other broadcasters, including internationally. BBC Studios represents the logic of vertical integration within an increasingly marketised public service model, with D'Arma (2017) arguing that this represents a 'hollowing out' of the publicly funded structures within UK broadcasting. Defending the commercial development of BBC Studios, the BBC Executive Committee countered:

> [O]wning content production and intellectual property ("IP") is vital if the BBC is to compete in an increasingly globalised market. The proposal aims to secure a stable source of content for the BBC, by offering greater creative and commercial freedom in order to attract talent. This would in turn generate sources of IP that can be exploited internationally, the resulting revenues being reinvested into content and services for UK licence fee payers. (Ofcom 2015, para 1.4)

Taken together, BBC Studios and its counterpart ITV Studios, represent a major new force in UK television production, raising significant questions about their commercial impact on the other major supplier of drama, namely the independent production sector.

Independent production companies have become central to the delivery of television content in the UK and globally. As discussed in the previous chapter, their ability to retain intellectual property rights for content (enshrined in the UK Communications Act 2003), coupled with favourable terms of trade and deregulation, can be credited with ensuring the sector's growth in the UK. In addition to this, a range of regulatory and policy changes (many instigated by 'New Labour' governments in the 1990s) and a climate of social change which transformed the structures of work and encouraged entrepreneurialism, created an environment conducive to the development of the independent production sector (Lee 2018). The growth of this sector ensured competition and provided diverse content for broadcasters, particularly Channel 4 and S4C whose own origins are deeply entwined in the development of the

---

[3] For this reason, it is unsurprising that Ofcom is planning a consultation on BBC Studios activity in 2019.

sector. This evolution has in turn impacted on the forms and characteristics of labour, as we will see in Chapter 5.

Among the UK's diverse independent production companies, only a modest number have developed specialisms in drama. Many of these have been acquired by larger, often global, companies. For example, Red Production Company was established in 1998 by Nicola Shindler as a talent-led company working closely with writers such as Sally Wainwright. Red has produced some of the UK's best-known dramas including *Happy Valley* (2014–present), *Last Tango in Halifax* (2012–2016), *Queer as Folk* (1999–2000) and *Scott and Bailey* (2011–2016). In 2013 Red Productions was acquired by StudioCanal, the production arm of Canal+, in its efforts to become the preeminent European distributor and producer of fictional film and television (Meir 2016).

Today, the UK independent production sector is strongly characterised by acquisitions and mergers, with consolidation focused at the mid-tier level. In his comparative study of UK and Spanish independent production companies, Fernández-Quijada (2013) points to the extent to which the UK ecology is shaped by internationalisation as a result of deregulation and the pursuit of greater efficiencies. Today, many specialist drama indies retain their identity but are part of much larger media groups. Kudos, the maker of *Spooks* (2002–2011), *Life on Mars* (2006–2007) and *Broadchurch* (2013–2017), is part of the global Endemol Shine Group, which comprises 120 companies across all the world's major media markets. Shed, another major producer of returning drama series including *Waterloo Road* (2006–2015) and *Footballers' Wives* (2002–2006), was acquired by Time Warner to form Warner Bros. Television Productions UK. This is part of a wider moment of change for the independent sector in the UK as it matures (see Lee 2018) and raises significant questions about anti-competitive effects resulting from this merger and acquisition activity in the global television sector (Evens and Donders 2016). The examples above illustrate that the UK is firmly in an era of 'super-indies' (Chalaby 2010) and even 'mega-indies' (Elwes 2015) in which major multinational production companies with significant global reach and resources are able to exercise increasing power in the television market begging the question of what indies are now independent from.

In 2017, PACT chief executive John McVay declared 'small' indies (with revenue up to £10 million) to be in rude health, yet paradoxically also revealed that while nearly 100 indies launch each year, around 50%

fail within two years (Lamarra 2018). This is a saturated market in which profit margins are squeezed and there is little funding available for initial idea development or radical experimentation. The strategic rationale is that large indies will be able to withstand some of this financial pressure and develop their own economies of scale, a requisite for any company wanting to make high-quality drama today.

A further change in the landscape is around the definition of 'independent'. In 2014 the UK government redefined 'independent' in the statutes, meaning that independent companies can be owned by a foreign broadcaster if this broadcaster is not directly trying to reach the British market. As Lee (2018, 177) concludes, 'This is a radically new interpretation of 'independent' by media policy-makers and represents a significant shift away from the early values and ethos of the indie sector, which was prized for its apparent independence from controlling corporate structures'. For example, all3Media is jointly owned by the US companies Discovery Communications and Liberty Global but the all3Media company covers a range of individual production labels and distributors. These companies include Bentley Productions and Neal Street Productions making content such as *Midsomer Murders* (1997–present), *Call the Midwife* (2012–present) and *Penny Dreadful* (2014–2016). In what has been termed 'The Great British TV sell-off' (Deans 2014) large swathes of the UK sector are now under the control of foreign owners, raising critical questions around the continued diversity, pluralism and innovation of the sector.

COMMISSIONING DRAMA

Though the precise structure of pitching systems varies between broadcasters, a further defining characteristic of UK drama is the power of a small number of London-based commissioners to decide what gets made. Commissioning editors form a well-established elite in television production, operating as an intermediary between the broadcast organisation and programme supplier. Their expert knowledge is based around a creative instinct which interprets audience tastes, attempts to predict demand and positions content; ultimately, commissioners act as broadcasters' investors in content and they are powerful gatekeepers. In the past two decades, they have also assumed an ambassadorial role, communicating the strategic direction and ambition of the broadcaster to a range of stakeholders at myriad industry events. While commissioners tend to work in isolation and often in competition with one another (Preston 2003, 4), they each have a team of staff acting as conduits with the independent sector from whence many pitches emerge. Commissioners in turn liaise with controllers who have oversight of content produced for a specific genre or for an entire channel. Indeed, the commissioning system entails careful collaboration between the controllers of individual channels and genre commissioners.

Access to drama commissioners is limited deliberately; most have pre-existing close relationships with key production companies, literary and screen agencies. Though in theory pitches are accepted from all-comers, in practice the opportunities for pitching are limited. This hierarchical system enforces gatekeeping and concentrates decision-making (and finance) to a small number of senior staff who may become successful career commissioners. These are prominent cultural intermediaries and highly mobile individuals who move routinely between commissioning roles, including to work in the US. They tend to be located near to the centre of their organisation and so commissioners are often concentrated in major production hubs such as London and Los Angeles often making it difficult for suppliers outside of these locales to gain access and build a professional relationship.

The prominence and homogeneity of a small number of drama commissioners, and the sway they hold in being able to commission what suits their taste, has long been a matter of heated debate within television production circles. An especially voluble critic has been Tony Garnett, the renowned director and producer of landmark dramas such as *Cathy Come Home* (1966), *Days of Hope* (1975), and *This Life* (1996–1997). He has argued that:

> The top brass – not only in the BBC – are hooked on the junk food of soaps and renewable one-hour series, which become formulaic and institutionalised, going on year after year. The writers work in a straitjacket. It's an efficient way for a programme controller to guarantee an audience, but the BBC should be more ambitious. (Garnett cited in Pells 2014)

Garnett is not alone in his criticisms. The BAFTA-award winning director Peter Kosminsky (*The Government Inspector* 2005; *Wolf Hall* 2015) used a speech at the Edinburgh Television Festival to identify the failings of the current drama commissioning system and the rift that he believes exists between commissioners and producers:

> They sit in their glass box meeting rooms, they don't mix with programme makers, they're often not programme makers themselves. [They] hive themselves off into ... I was going to say 'ivory towers' but they're glass towers normally ... programme makers are perceived as the enemy by the commissioners and commissioners are perceived as the enemy by the programme makers. (Kosminsky cited in Holmes 2015)

For such critics, drama commissioning seems like a thoroughly commercial 'command and control' structure. A ratings-led approach, critics argue, reduces the creative autonomy of programme makers and shifts control to risk-averse, office-based staff who have limited interactions with those making the programmes they commission. In the process, the distinctive nature of public service broadcasting, they fear, is being eroded, most especially its capacity to take risks and address major social and political moments of change by speaking to viewers ostensibly as fellow citizens rather than as consumers:

> The BBC, particularly in drama, should be doing something no-one else does, and no-one else can do: making programmes that make things hot for people in power, and rocking the boat. Not just politicians but all people who are generally unassailable and comfortable in their fat cat positions. (Kosminsky cited in Khan 2009)

From the perspective of commissioners, however, the political attack on public service broadcasting is itself one of the reasons for being cautious in their allocation of public funding. Scrutiny of PSBs is now so intense that commissioners are concerned not to risk the reputation of the broadcasters through, for example, spending large sums of funding on what may turn out to be a 'flop'. As Doyle argues, looked at from the vantage of media economics, 'a key objective for content creation businesses is to establish operating conditions that are conducive to production of regular hits and that enable effective management of failure' (Doyle 2016, 36). To be associated with the commissioning of an unsuccessful drama carries both institutional and professional risk.

The shift in power from producers to commissioners has a long history intimately tied to the deregulation of broadcasting in the UK. It is this which lends this debate its ideological edge. As Bignell and Lacey argue:

The use of temporary contracts and the outsourcing of production to independent producers, and the introduction of an internal market at the BBC, have shifted decision-making powers from programme-makers to schedulers and commissioners and made the career paths of programme-makers much more unstable. When John Birt led the BBC in the 1990s the sweeping changes he introduced weakened the independence of the producer by centralising power in London and giving more control to commissioners, schedulers and controllers. (Bignell and Lacey 2014, 10–11)

For some critics, the geographical concentration of commissioners also explains the relative lack of dramas based in and reflective of the diverse regions and nations of the UK. In an unusually candid essay for the Royal Television Society, Jane Tranter, the BBC's former Controller of Drama Commissioning (2000–2009), reflected on how, in the early years of her tenure, she lacked the open-mindedness to see that:

[I]t was the attitude of the BBC towards Wales that was the problem, not the place itself. All it took was to give Wales a chance. The experience of filming in Wales the first five seasons of the rebooted *Doctor Who* was challenging, joyous, creative and productive. (RTS 2016)

If first-hand experience can radically alter a commissioner's perspective, it is vital that public broadcasters ensure they have commissioners embedded in different production centres across the UK. As Tranter went on to argue, if the PSBs 'are to continue to benefit from the regions they film in, they must take more care and responsibility for their development and sustainability. Planning their commissioning commitments would be a big step forward'. The call to relocate at least some commissioners to UK regions and nations extends the earlier BBC strategy of decentralising television production away from London and the south-east of England (Noonan 2012). This is very much an ongoing debate with the commercially funded public broadcaster Channel 4 due to move part of its headquarters to Leeds, with additional production hubs opening in Glasgow and Bristol. This relocation is intended to decentralise permanently decision-making in order to distribute resources, spread benefits and ensure more diversity on and off-screen—themes we will pick up again in the next chapter.

The narrowness of the commissioning process has also been criticised in terms of diversity. For example, the actor Idris Elba, who has spoken openly about needing to move to the US to get more interesting roles as a black actor, argues:

> [T]he Britain I come from is the most successful, diverse, multicultural country on earth. But here's my point: you wouldn't know it if you turned on the TV. Too many of our creative decision-makers share the same background ... Too often commissioners look at diverse talent, and all they see is risk. Black actors are seen as a commercial risk. Women directors are seen as a commercial risk. Disabled directors aren't even seen at all. In general, if broadcasters want to stay in the game, their commissioners must take more risk with diverse talent. (Elba cited in Channel 4 2016)

Speaking to members of parliament about the issue, Elba advocated three ways to bring about change:

1. A change of mindset: get all commissioners and content creators to think about diversifying at the beginning of the creative process, not the end.
2. Transparency: friendly competition between broadcasters. See who's actually doing the best creative diversity. Benchmark it. That encourages everyone to do better.
3. A different approach towards risk. The story of Netflix is that risk-taking delivers audiences. (Elba cited in Channel 4 2016)

While the diversity of controllers and commissioners need not in itself bring about direct change to what or who appears on screen (see Saha 2012), Elba's argument about risk being an inhibitor is well made.

THE PITCH AND THE MONEY

Most new television dramas begin life as a pitch. Exceptionally established writers and producers regarded as proven 'talent' may approach a commissioner directly with an idea for a drama. In the US, these people are normally described as 'showrunners' and they are regarded as the creative fulcrum of drama production worthy not only of industry but fan adulation as in the case, for example, of Joss Whedon, whose credits included *Buffy the Vampire Slayer* (1997–2003) and *Agents of S.H.I.E.L.D.* (2013–present) among others. The showrunner model of drama production has spread beyond the US, as Eva Novrup Redvall (2013) has demonstrated in her analysis of Danish drama production. Whether as cause or by-product of the rise of cinematic television, the showrunner has increasingly been regarded as the medium's *auteur* whose distinct vision holds together franchises that cross platforms and which are written by teams of writers. Critically assessing the showrunner as a historically specific formation of the auteur, Elizabeth Blakeley points to the likes of David Benioff and D. B. Weiss, showrunners of *Game of Thrones* (2011–present), as examples 'of how world-building narratives, found in other media such as novels, can be produced and distributed on TV, in ways not conceivable during the broadcast era' (2017, 327). In the UK, scholars Matt Hills (2014) and James Chapman (forthcoming) have named writers such as Russell T. Davies, Chris Chibnall and Steven Moffat as showrunners whose distinct signature can be discerned on screen in their narrative and style.

Nonetheless, the showrunner production model is still less common in drama production in the UK. The more common route is for a one-page proposal or pitch to be sent to a drama commissioning executive from a producer, often at an independent production company with whom there will be an established networking relationship. As most commissioners will only buy a handful of brand-new drama series each year, they offer clear guides to those wishing to pitch to them, as illustrated by ITV drama's commissioning brief:

> We are looking for clear ideas which can deliver the highest quality popular mainstream drama to the largest audience. No subject is off-limits – we can rise to celebratory, hilarious highs or plunge to very dark areas of human behaviour. But we will always look for mainstream appeal and an accessible way in for our audience. … An ITV drama is never cynical and is always entertaining, and even in the darkest stories we seek the hope of redemption. We don't do black comedy or satire, and we can't be bleak. (ITV 2018a)

Proposals received by the commissioners will likely include a title, log line (a one- or two-sentence summary) and an overview of the structure of the drama; it will make a case for the timeliness of the project, its channel suitability, and will identify a potential audience and a suggested slot within the schedule. It will also normally include a plot summary, a succinct description of the lead characters and any major talent likely to be attached. If it is a series rather than a one-off, there will also be brief episode summaries. If the pitch is not rejected, extended treatments and follow-up meetings will take place between the producers and commissioning executives, potentially leading to a first tier of finance being released to support first-draft script development or even a rough pilot episode. If these are well-received, many subsequent draft scripts will be produced with a great deal of to-ing and fro-ing between the writer(s), producers and drama commissioning executives. This process can take many months or years before a full pilot episode or series may be commissioned and a further tranche of funding released by the broadcaster to the production company. PSBs make public the price ranges which they will pay for an hour of a particular programme and these prices vary significantly between broadcasters as illustrated in Table 3.1 with reference to the tariffs for BBC and S4C drama commissions. The 'tariff prices', as they are commonly known, are dependent on genre of programming and are included within the Code of Practice of the broadcasters (Table 3.2).

These tariffs demonstrate the considerable variation in price offered to different types of drama. They also reveal the hierarchies extant in drama production.

If a series is finally commissioned by a broadcaster, a production schedule and detailed budget will be produced, and the process of casting and assembling a production crew will begin. At this point, another substantial tranche of funding is likely to be released as filming takes place, normally over a limited and tightly planned period of a few weeks. Post-production will follow with viewings of rushes and subsequent edits being reviewed not only by the director(s) but also by the executive producers, most commonly comprising the head of the independent production company and the drama controller at the broadcaster. At the point of delivery of the final edit in approved technical conditions, the last tranche of funding will be released to the production company as the publicity team prepares to market the drama ahead of broadcast.

While viewers are increasingly turning to catch-up services, television schedules continue to have strategic value to broadcasters (Bruun 2018; Ihlebæk et al. 2014; Van den Bulck and Enli 2014). Live viewing remains the most common way in which television is consumed, especially at key times of the year (Ofcom 2018b). The schedule, therefore, is a vital part of the commissioning process. As ITV explains, 'While finding returnable series is a priority, we also need two, three and four parters, ideally with the potential to return though not exclusively.

Table 3.1   BBC tariff range of indicative prices for the supply of commissioned television programmes

Network drama: £50k–£1000k per hour
Nations and regions drama: £30k–£450k per hour

This indicative tariff range covers a wide variety of programming, from low cost daytime output to high-end landmark series. Programmes will tend to fall into the following categories:

Category	Specifications	Tariff (£k per hour)
Low cost drama	Low cost output primarily for daytime together with long-running series (soaps) for BBC One and BBC Two	50–600
Mid-range drama	Series and serials with high production values and known talent	500–800
Premium drama	Premium drama series, serials or one-offs. They will include a combination of multilocation, high cast, period setting, CGI, effects and stunts	650–1000
Nations and regions drama	Applies to all nations and regions drama and includes short film development	30–450

Source BBC (2019a)

Table 3.2   S4C 2013 tariff range for commissioned drama

Drama	Tariff—cost per hour
Contemporary drama series	
The licence fee will depend on location, number of characters, script requirements, etc.	£100,000–£200,000 per hour
Period drama series	
The licence fee will depend on location, number of characters, script requirements, etc.	£110,000–£240,000 per hour
Other drama series	
Drama series with a lower cost due to factors such as the number of episodes, size of cast, a limited number of locations and filming methods	£75,000–£120,000 per hour
Situation comedy/studio drama	£75,000–£130,000 per hour
Single drama	
The licence fee will depend on the cost of talent, programme length, period of the drama as well as the number and the nature of the locations	Subject to discussion depending on the script requirements and nature of the production

Source S4C (2013)

We also need one-off films to be Bank Holiday specials' (ibid.). There is enduring interest in Christmas schedules and festive episodes of popular dramas such as *Doctor Who* and *Call the Midwife*. Strategic use of schedules is also a way of partially combatting piracy, especially important to drama as high-profile series are the most likely to be shared illegally online. Broadcasters have attempted to overcome this by broadcasting major dramas like *Game of Throne* and *Twin Peaks* (1990–1991, 2017) simultaneously across different territories and time zones in an effort to create television 'events' and to ensure rights owners retain more international value.

One of the biggest changes in television drama production has been the shift in financing (Hammett-Jamart 2018; Raats et al. 2016; Steemers 2016). Today, UK broadcasters almost never fund any drama fully, instead offering in multiple tiered stages something closer to two-thirds of production costs. This is referred to as a 'deficit model'. The remainder of the funding comes from a mixture of external sources, including funding secured by the independent production companies themselves via the marketplace; co-production finance which is often international and, increasingly, may also come in the form of an equity share from distributors such as BBC Worldwide or all3Media; public finance from regional or national funds; or through sources such as the MEDIA subprogramme of Creative Europe which financially supports the development, distribution and promotion of European content. Drama is very much a global business, therefore co-production finance, 'in association with', acquisitions and distribution deals are all vital to getting a series 'greenlit'.

Co-production is a prominent feature of the production ecology for drama content. For example, about two-thirds of the BBC's TV drama is funded by commercial deals (Public Accounts Committee 2018). Co-production allows partners to share some of the risk and to fulfil some of the creative expectations surrounding drama today. The British version of the sci-fi drama *Humans* (2015–present), based on the Swedish series, *Äkta människor* (2012–2014), was developed initially by the independent producer Kudos for Channel 4 alone but ultimately became a co-production with the US network AMC, as leveraging extra investment from the US enhanced the scale and production values of the show. As Channel 4's head of drama at the time reflected, 'To put it bluntly, it allowed us to do robots well … Making sci-fi work for a mainstream audience, at 9 pm, meant rendering it so that it didn't feel in any way homemade' (Piers Wenger cited in Midgley 2016).

While co-production alleviates some of the financial pressures, independent production companies in the UK still carry much of the risk when making drama. Indeed, data from PACT in 2015 shows a significant increase in indies' estimated contribution to production finance, particularly in terms of gap financing (i.e. where the primary commission is less than the direct costs of the programme) (Conlan 2015). The pay-off, however, is that indies retain the rights after primary transmission and commercial holdback (normally two years) so they can, for instance, sell secondary rights to other UK broadcasters, DVD distributors and international broadcasters. The emergence of niche digital channels showing drama re-runs provides a lucrative market. For example, UKTV is an independent commercial joint venture between BBC Worldwide and Discovery, Inc which has among its portfolio two channels, Gold and Drama, that are described on the company's website as 'curating brand-defining commissions, high-profile acquisitions and the very best of BBC, alongside programmes originally shown on ITV and Channel 4'. Moreover, British drama production increasingly operates in an international finance environment which allows rights holders to retain a large proportion of secondary and ancillary rights of their productions as a way of covering the funding gap (Fernández-Quijada 2013, 115). This model distinguishes UK television production from much of Europe and underscores the current ecology, revenue patterns, and balance of risk in drama production.

Less common in the drama market is the sale of formats—a key point of distinction from the distribution of entertainment content. Transnational drama formats may be more or less open to creative innovation (see Hilmes 2012) with franchises such as *Law and Order: UK* (2009–2014) being tightly controlled by the US parent company, Wolf Films, while British series *Skins* (2007–2013) and *Shameless* (2004–2013) have both been remade for US audiences. However, a remarkably successful example of UK drama formatting is *Doc Martin* (2004–present). This popular comic rural medical drama, set in a photogenic Cornwall location, has been aired since 2004 on ITV. In addition to enjoying frequent re-runs and a prominent place on ITV Hub (the broadcaster's online player), *Doc Martin* has also been sold to more than 70 territories and has been remade in countries such as

France, Germany, Greece and Spain, making considerable profits for Buffalo Pictures, the independent production company formed in 1996 by Philippa Braithwaite and Martin Clunes, who plays the eponymous lead character. While the basic ingredients of the drama remain consistent, the national remakes exemplify the process of 'glocalisation' (the localisation of globally traded content to suit local markets and cultural tastes). For example, the Greek version called *Clinical Cases* (*Kliniki Periptosi*) has Markos Staikos in the lead role as a surgeon returning to a small Greek village from New York, while the German version, *Doktor Martin*, more closely follows the original with Dr. Martin Helling, a vascular surgeon from the city (Berlin rather than London) who, like Martin Clunes' character, is afraid of blood. The French version exploits some of the distinct transnational connections between Celtic locales, with Dr. Martin Le Foll arriving in the fictional Breton town of Port-Garrec, twinned with the Cornish Portwenn of the original series. The format hinges on comic clashes between the outsider doctor and his patients in a quirky, parochial community that nonetheless welcomes the outsider (most obviously through romances with one or more local women); *Doc Martin* and its remakes testify to the complex local-national-transnational axis along which contemporary television drama travels.

Disrupting Distribution

Compared to the sale of formats, the international sale of UK programmes has far more financial significance. Finished content accounts for 50% of UK indies' revenue from rights, delivering £166m in revenue to producers in 2016 and growing over 13% between 2010 and 2016 (PACT 2017b, 10). ITV's historical drama *Victoria* (2016–present) is just one example that illustrates the global mobility and enduring value of content. Domestically the first series was the channel's highest-rated drama of 2016, with the second series securing a consolidated average of 6.4 million viewers and a 25% share of the UK audience (ITV 2018b). The series, produced by drama specialist Mammoth Screen (a subsidiary of ITV Studios) as a co-production with the US broadcaster PBS, has also been hugely popular in the US with the second series reaching an average of 5.2m viewers on PBS as part of its Masterpiece strand. The series has been further sold to 189 countries worldwide, as negotiated by the distributor ITV Studios Global Entertainment.

A dynamic network of content distributors like ITV Studios exists to facilitate the sale of television content from one territory to another. The globalisation of television drama production has amplified the significance of distributors in this ecology and helps explain why both BBC and ITV have developed their international distribution arms. Distributors operate as intermediaries, licensing either their own and/or third-party content, formats and content-related rights to a range of buyers including broadcasters, consumer product licensees and SVoD services (Steemers 2016). They provide valuable international market intelligence to commissioners and producers which is both economic and cultural in nature and they are increasingly significant conduits for local productions to be seen internationally. They operate as routes to export and are especially important as a source of future revenues and not least because the UK, unlike the US, does not have a broadcast syndication system. More recently, these content distributors have also become a significant source of financing within the structures of television production. For example, all3Media comprises 18 production companies from across the world, each of which operates as their own businesses, retaining their own 'distinctive creative signature'. The Welsh dramas *Craith/Hidden* (2018–present) and *Y Gwyll/Hinterland* (2013–present) both received support from all3Media International, which secured sales for both series across Europe, the US and the Asia Pacific region. Amanda Rees, Director of Creative Content at S4C, which premiered the Welsh version of the series, noted:

> S4C has striven to commission drama with genuine universality – through stories that are rooted in our unique Welsh culture and landscape. We are delighted that, through the efforts of all3media international, *Craith/Hidden* and indeed *Y Gwyll/Hinterland* are traveling the world so successfully. (all3Media International 2018)

In drama, distributors can often provide bridge financing of between 20 and 30%, thereby assuming significantly greater risk than in the past and demonstrating the change from distributors as salespeople to also being financiers (Steemers 2016, 747).[4]

---

[4] A producer will seek 'bridge financing' when filming has begun but the production loan has yet to release funds.

It is not only the role of distributors that is evolving. A major concern for both broadcasters and producers is how new funding agreements are affecting rights ownership, and therefore the ability of producers to exploit fully the economic value of their own content (Doyle 2016). The arrival of new SVoD buyers (still few in number in the UK, but set to rise) offers a broader market for indies with content to sell. On the one hand, this may be looked upon positively, as the PACT 'UK Television Exports' report affirms:

> This year's survey highlighted the increasing importance of digital rights particularly on SVOD platforms such as Netflix and Amazon. Respondents believe that there is further opportunity for growth from this area. (PACT 2017a, 3)

Foremost, these platforms provide the possibility of global distribution. They have access to more financial resources and so are often able to pay significantly more than their rivals for content, especially publicly funded broadcasters. There is prestige and brand value for indies in producing a Netflix original series which will sit alongside hugely successful content such as *Stranger Things* (2016–present) and *The Crown* (2016–present). On the other hand, the patterns for exploiting intellectual property through secondary rights are constrained. Unlike PSBs who operate on a 'deficit model' (outlined above), SVoDs generally commission on a 'cost-plus system'. This means that while they meet all production costs, they also retain all rights. This has a significant impact on territoriality (licensing content in different geographic territories) and windowing (licensing content for distribution on different platforms often with staggered timescales)—two strategies which have been the cornerstones of the business model of television distribution (Steemers 2016). Under the terms of the arrangement with a company like Netflix, the producer will have to wait a certain period of time before it licenses the show elsewhere (sometimes up to 10 years). On top of this, the global expansion of Netflix into more than 190 countries means that few local broadcasters would be prepared to pay large amounts for content that is available on the Netflix service. This presents a 'conundrum' (Patel 2018) for independent producers and other rights owners as they consider the cost of exclusivity and the loss of ancillary revenue streams from licensing and merchandising. While the likes of Netflix and Amazon Prime may bring substantial new opportunities for production in the present, their use of the cost-plus finance model will greatly inhibit indies in exploiting their intellectual property in the longer term. As Doyle's (2016) research on UK distribution reveals, the national model of commissioning television is being challenged by the global financing model of profit-driven SVoDs whose largely unregulated business models drive them to accumulate IP assets from the territories in which they operate.

We argue that this is a major evolution from existing transnational flows of programming as detailed by scholars like Weissmann (2012) and Hilmes (2012). SVoDs operate on a global rights model that leverages their capital assets and reach in order to negotiate exceptional mobility across territories. This is clearly already an area of concern for some in UK television:

> In the past distribution and rights businesses were built on rights to a territory and particular segments of rights for that territory and particular windows ... Now the Netflix's are going "Right let's just scrap the territory model" ... Multi-territory global buyers are completely changing the landscape ... It reduces potential revenues. It makes it a lot more difficult because a buyer will now say "Well, you are making it for me in country X but I want to use this in countries Y and Z." You will find some way of making them pay something for that, but very rarely will it be what you would have got if you had taken it to them directly after the event and it will be certainly a lot less than what you would have got if you had been able to generate competition for the rights to the particular product created. So, it is bad news. (Doyle 2016, 638, citing interview with the CCO of Warner Bros. International Television)

While SVoD and telecommunications firms are heralded as major disruptors in television distribution, larger PSBs are also responding to new opportunities to exploit rights internationally and to distribute content to distinct transnational audience segments. The launch of Britbox, the digital video subscription service from BBC Studios and ITV plc, illustrates some of that response. But while initiatives like this do speak to an ambition to be innovative and international, PSBs are still subject to much more stringent regulation and public criticism of their digital strategies. For early 2019, the BBC proposed a number of changes to its iPlayer service 'to transform iPlayer, from primarily a catch-up and linear TV service into a destination for our audiences, where the BBC's programmes will be available for longer, both for individual programmes and box sets' (BBC 2019b). However, the regulator Ofcom regarded these as material changes to the BBC's UK Public Services and so the BBC undertook a Public Interest Test, an evidence-based process used to assess the public value of a change and its impact on competition. At the time of writing the outcome of this test had not been published but for us, the process speaks to the regulatory scrutiny that PSBs face, while SVoD companies face precious little intervention.

This chapter has mapped the complex and shifting ecology of television drama production in the UK, revealing both the specific and historic characteristics of the PSB/indie relationship and the major disruptions to that relationship which new entrants and services pose. Broad trends in the industry combine with government policy-making to determine the likely sustainability of the industry and the shape of what we see on screen. In the next chapter, we extend our analysis to examine broader cultural and economic expectations in relation to local production in this global era of drama production.

References

all3media International. 'Hidden Reveals Itself to North America, EMEA and Asia Pacific'. *all3media International,* 14 May 2018. Accessed 9 July 2018. https://www.all3mediainternational.com/News/Article/55?pageFrom=0&pageId=0.

BBC. 'BBC Worldwide and BBC Studios to Join Forces as Single Commercial Organisation'. 29 November 2017. Accessed 13 March 2019. https://www.bbc.co.uk/mediacentre/latestnews/2017/studios-worldwide.

BBC (a). 'Programme Prices and Tariff Ranges'. Commissioning, 2019. Accessed 30 March 2019. https://www.bbc.co.uk/commissioning/tv/articles/how-we-do-business#schedule-of-residuals.

BBC (b). 'Public Interest Test Consultation on BBC iPlayer Proposals'. 7 January 2019. Accessed 13 March 2019. https://www.bbc.co.uk/aboutthebbc/insidethebbc/howwework/accountability/consultations/bbc-iplayer-public-interest.

BBC Trust. 'Window of Creative Competition for Television'. March 2013. Accessed 24 March 2019. http://downloads.bbc.co.uk/bbctrust/assets/files/pdf/review_report_research/wocc_third/wocc_third.pdf.

Bignell, Jonathan and Stephen Lacey. *British Television Drama: Past, Present and Future.* 2nd edition. Basingstoke: Palgrave Macmillan, 2014.

Blakeley, Elizabeth. 'Showrunner as Auteur: Bridging the Culture/Economy Binary in Digital Hollywood'. *Open Cultural Studies* 1, 1 (2017): 321–332.

Bruun, Hanne. 'Producing the On-Air Schedule in Danish Public Service Television in the Digital Era'. *Critical Studies in Television* 13, 2 (2018): 137–152.

Chalaby, Jean. 'The Rise of Britain's Super-Indies: Policy-Making in the Age of the Global Media Market'. *International Communication Gazette* 72, 8 (2010): 675–693.

Channel 4. 'Idris Elba's Keynote Speech to Parliament on Diversity in the Media'. 18 January 2016. Accessed 8 July 2018. http://www.channel4.com/info/press/news/idris-elba-s-keynote-speech-to-parliament-on-diversity-in-the-media.

Chapman, James. *Contemporary British Television Drama*. London: I.B. Tauris, forthcoming.

Conlan, Tara. 'Indie TV Producers Forced to Take Bigger Risks as Cutbacks Bite'. *The Guardian*, 16 August 2015. Accessed 24 August 2018. https://www.theguardian.com/media/2015/aug/16/indie-tv-producers-funding-gap.

D'Arma, Alessandro. 'The Hollowing Out of Public Service Media: A Constructivist Institutionalist Analysis of the Commercialisation of BBC's In-House Production'. *Media, Culture and Society* 40, 3 (2017): 432–448.

Deans, Jason. 'The Great British TV Sell-Off: What Do Foreign Companies Own?' *The Guardian*, 30 October 2014. Accessed 23 August 2018. https://www.theguardian.com/media/2014/oct/30/the-great-british-tv-sell-off-what-do-foreign-companies-own.

Doyle, Gillian. 'Digitization and Changing Windowing Strategies in the Television Industry: Negotiating New Windows on the World'. *Television and New Media* 17, 7 (2016): 629–645.

Elwes, Tabitha. 'The Rise of the Mega-Indie'. *Broadcast*, 26 March 2015. Accessed 21 August 2018. https://www.broadcastnow.co.uk/the-rise-of-the-mega-indie/5085614.article.

Evens, Tom and Karen Donders. 'Mergers and Acquisitions in TV Broadcasting and Distribution: Challenges for Competition, Industrial and Media Policy'. *Telematics and Informatics* 33, 2 (2016): 674–682.

Fernández-Quijada, David. 'Transnationalism and Media Groups in Independent Television Production in the UK and Spain'. *Global Media and Communication* 9, 2 (2013): 101–118.

Hammett-Jamart, Julia, Petar Mitric and Eva Novrup Redvall (eds). *European Film and Television Co-production: Policy and Practice*. Basingstoke: Palgrave Macmillan, 2018.

Hills, Matt. 'Hyping Who and Marketing the Steven Moffat Era: The Role of 'Prior Paratexts'. In *Doctor Who The Eleventh Hour: A Critical Celebration of the Matt Smith and Steven Moffat Era*, edited by Andrew O'Day, 181–203. London: I.B. Tauris, 2014.

Hilmes, Michele. 'The Whole World's Unlikely Heroine: Ugly Betty as Transnational Phenomenon'. In *Reading Ugly Betty: TV's Betty Goes Global*, edited by Janet McCabe and Kim Akass, 26–44. London: I.B. Taurus, 2012.

Holmes, Jonathan. '"Commissioning Is Broken" Says the Director of Wolf Hall'. *Radio Times*, 27 August 2015. Accessed 8 July 2018. https://www.radiotimes.com/news/2015-08-27/commissioning-is-broken-says-the-director-of-wolf-hall/.

Ihlebæk, Karoline Andrea, Trine Syvertsen and Espen Ytreberg. 'Keeping Them and Moving Them: TV Scheduling in the Phase of Channel and Platform Proliferation'. *Television & New Media* 15, 5 (2014): 470–486.

ITV (a). 'Commissioning: Drama'. 2018. Accessed 8 July 2018. http://www.itv.com/commissioning/drama.

ITV (b). 'Filming Commences on the Third Series of ITV's Victoria'. *ITV Press Centre*, 1 May 2018. Accessed 8 July 2018. https://www.itv.com/presscentre/press-releases/filming-commences-third-series-itvs-victoria.

Khan, Urmee. 'Director Peter Kosminsky Launches Attack on BBC Drama'. *The Telegraph*, 17 March 2009. Accessed 2 July 2018. https://www.telegraph.co.uk/culture/tvandradio/5001773/Director-Peter-Kosminsky-launches-attack-on-BBC-drama.html.

Lamarra, Ian. 'Indies Face Fight to Survive'. Broadcast, 14 February 2018. Accessed 23 August 2018. https://www.broadcastnow.co.uk/indies/indies-face-fight-to-survive/5126520.article.

Lee, David. *Independent Television Production in the UK: From Cottage Industry to Big Business*. Cham, Switzerland: Palgrave Macmillan, 2018.

McElroy, Ruth and Caitriona Noonan. 'Television Drama Production in Small Nations: Mobilities in a Changing Ecology'. *Journal of Popular Television* 4, 1 (2016): 109–127.

Meir, Christopher. 'Studiocanal and the Changing Industrial Landscape of European Cinema and Television'. *Media Industries* 3, 1 (2016). http://dx.doi.org/10.3998/mij.15031809.0003.104.

Midgley, Neil. 'Selling War and Peace to the Russians: Global Cash Drives UK Drama'. *The Guardian*, 21 February 2016. Accessed 8 July 2018. https://www.theguardian.com/media/2016/feb/21/tv-drama-global-war-peace-missing?utm_source=twitterfeed&utm_medium=twitter.

Noonan, Caitriona. 'The BBC and Decentralisation: The Pilgrimage to Manchester'. *International Journal of Cultural Policy* 18, 4 (2012): 363–377.

Ofcom. 'BBC Content Production Options'. 23 December 2015. Accessed 22 August 2018. https://www.ofcom.org.uk/__data/assets/pdf.../bbc-content_production_options.pdf.

Ofcom (a). 'Media Nations: UK 2018'. 18 July 2018. Accessed 22 August 2018. https://www.ofcom.org.uk/research-and-data/tv-radio-and-on-demand/media-nations.

Ofcom (b). 'Communications Market Report 2017'. 17 August 2018. Accessed 21 August 2018. https://www.ofcom.org.uk/research-and-data/multi-sector-research/cmr/cmr-2017.

PACT (a). 'UK Television Exports 2015–2016'. 3 February 2017. Accessed 24 August 2018. http://www.pact.co.uk/news-detail.html?id=impressive-growth-in-uk-television-exports-up-10-to-1-326m.

PACT (b). 'UK Television Production Survey: Financial Census 2017'. 5 September 2017. Accessed 24 August 2018. http://www.pact.co.uk/news-detail.html?id=international-revenues-continue-to-drive-growth-in-the-uk-tv-production-sector.

Patel, Sahil. 'Netflix's Deal Terms Pose a Conundrum for TV Studios'. 19 March 2018. Accessed 24 August 2018. https://digiday.com/media/netflixs-deal-terms-pose-a-conundrum-for-tv-studios/.

Pells, Rachael. 'Junk Television Stifles Creativity, Producer Tony Garnett Tells BBC'. *Independent*, 16 November 2014. Accessed 8 July 2018. http://www.independent.co.uk/arts-entertainment/tv/news/junk-television-stifles-creativity-producer-tony-garnett-tells-bbc-9863414.html.

Preston, Alison. *Inside the Commissioners: The Culture and Practice of Commissioning at UK Broadcasters.* Glasgow: The Research Centre for Television and Interactivity, 2003.

Public Accounts Committee. 'BBC Commercial Activities'. HC, June 2018, para 23. https://publications.parliament.uk/pa/cm201719/cmselect/cmpubacc/670/67002.htm.

Raats, Tim, Tom Evens and Sanne Ruelens. 'Challenges for Sustaining Local Audiovisual Ecosystems: Analysis of Financing and Production of Domestic TV Fiction in Small Media Markets'. *Journal of Popular Television* 4, 1 (2016): 129–147.

Redvall, Eva Novrup. *Writing and Producing Television Drama in Denmark: From The Kingdom to The Killing.* Basingstoke: Palgrave Macmillan, 2013.

RTS. 'Jane Tranter: Give Wales a Chance'. *RTS*, October 2016. Accessed 8 July 2018. https://rts.org.uk/article/jane-tranter-give-wales-chance.

S4C. 'Programme Tariffs—Cost Per Hour'. 18 June 2013. Accessed 30 March 2019. https://dlo6cycw1kmbs.cloudfront.net/media/media_assets/e_tariffau-mehefin-20132.pdf.

Saha, Anamik. '"Beards, Scarves, Halal Meat, Terrorists, Forced Marriage": Television Industries and the Production of "Race"'. *Media, Culture & Society* 34, 4 (2012): 424–438.

Slattery, Laura. 'RTÉ Issues Proclamation on Irish Drama'. *The Irish Times*, 7 January 2016. Accessed 25 May 2018. http://www.irishtimes.com/business/media-and-marketing/rt%C3%A9-issues-proclamation-on-irish-drama-1.2486729.

Steemers, Jeanette. 'International Sales of UK Television Content: Change and Continuity in "The Space in Between" Production and Consumption'. *Television and New Media* 17, 8 (2016): 734–753.

Stewart, Mark. 'The Myth of Televisual Ubiquity'. *Television & New Media* 17, 8 (2016): 691–705.

Van Den Bulck, Hilde and Gunn Sara Enli. 'Flow Under Pressure: Television Scheduling and Continuity Techniques as Victims of Media Convergence?' *Television and New Media* 15, 5 (2014): 441–452.

Weissmann, Elke. *Transnational Television Drama: Special Relations and Mutual Influences Between the US and the UK*. Abingdon and New York: Palgrave Macmillan, 2012.

Filmography

Agents of S.H.I.E.L.D (Marvel Television & Mutant Enemy Productions 2013–present).

Äkta människor (Sveriges Television (SVT), Matador Films 2012–2014).

Broadchurch (Kudos Film and Television, Imaginary Friends, ITV—Independent Television 2013–2017).

Buffy the Vampire Slayer (Mutant Enemy/Kuzui Enterprises/Sandollar Television/20th Century Fox Television 1997–2003).

Call the Midwife (Neal Street Productions/British Broadcasting Corporation 2012–present).

Casualty (British Broadcasting Corporation 1986–present).

Cathy Come Home (British Broadcasting Corporation 1966).

Craith/Hidden (Severn Screen 2018–present).

Crown, The (Left Bank Pictures/Sony Pictures Television Production UK 2016–present).

Days of Hope (British Broadcasting Corporation/Polytel 1975).

Doc Martin (Buffalo Pictures/Homerun Productions 2004–present).

Doctor Who (BBC Wales 2005–present).

Downton Abbey (Carnival Films/ITV Studios 2010–2015).

Footballers' Wives (Carlton Television/Shed Productions 2002–2006).

Game of Thrones (Home Box Office (HBO)/Television 360/Grok! Studio/ Generator Entertainment/Bighead Littlehead 2011–2019).

Government Inspector, The (Arte France/Mentorn Television/Stonehenge Films 2005).

Happy Valley (Red Production 2014–present).

Humans (Channel 4/Kudos/AMC 2015–present).

Last Tango in Halifax (Red Production Company/British Broadcasting Corporation 2012–2016).

Law and Order: UK (Kudos Film and TV/Wolf Films/NBC Universal Television/Universal Media Studies (UMS) 2009–2014).

Life on Mars (Kudos Film and Television/British Broadcasting Corporation/Red Planet Pictures 2006–2007).

Midsomer   Murders   (Bentley   Productions/ITV—Independent   Productions 1997–present).

Night Manager, The (BBC/AMC/The Ink Factory/Demarest Films/Character 7/Producciones Fortaleza AIE 2016).

Penny Dreadful (Desert Wolf Productions/Neal Street Productions 2014–2016).

Queer as Folk (Red Production Company 1999–2000).

Sarah Jane Adventures, The (BBC Wales 2007–2011).

Scott and Bailey (Red Production Company/Ingenious Broadcasting/Veredus Productions/Ipomen Productions 2011–2016).

Shameless (Company Pictures 2004–2013).

Sherlock (Hartswood Films 2010–present).

Skins (Company Pictures 2007–2013).

Spooks (Kudos Film and Television 2002–2011).

Stranger   Things   (21   Laps   Entertainment/Monkey   Massacre/Netflix 2016–present).

This Life (British Broadcasting Corporation/World Productions 1996–1997).

Torchwood (BBC Wales/Canadian Broadcasting Company/BBC Worldwide Productions 2006–2011).

Twin Peaks (Lynch/Frost Productions/Propaganda Films/Spelling Entertainment/ Twin Peaks Productions 1990–1991, 2017).

Victoria (Mammoth Screen/Masterpiece 2016–present).

War and Peace (BBC Cymru Wales/BBC Worldwide/Lookout Point 2016).

Waterloo   Road   (Shed   Productions/British   Broadcasting   Corporation 2006–2015).

Wolf Hall (Company Pictures/Playground Entertainment/British Broadcasting Corporation/Master Theatre/Hindsight Media 2015).

Y Gwyll/Hinterland (Fiction Factory 2015–present).

CHAPTER 4

Locating Regional Production

Abstract This chapter argues for the significance of regional television drama production, offering a critical paradigm for understanding the intersection of the local and global in TV production. Television drama's significance lies partly in how it locates itself in different cultural geographies, economic landscapes and sociolinguistic communities. For both broadcasters and audiences, drama's cultural value is closely associated with its representational power to visualise distinct locales and the people and stories which make places meaningful and diverse. Focusing on UK public service broadcasting, this chapter demonstrates how the appearance of certain places on screen is not a matter of happenstance but is rather the product of myriad policy, commercial, regulatory and creative decisions. Place is examined in three contexts: firstly, as a feature of the regulatory and structural organisation of UK production; secondly, in relation to the specific public purposes of the BBC as the UK's largest public service broadcaster and commissioner of television drama; and thirdly, as a quality marker of creative production, the effects of which are discernible visually *and* aurally on screen.

Keywords Place · Policy · Crime drama · Devolution ·
Production quotas · Landscape · Language · 'Lift and shift'

© The Author(s) 2019   73
R. McElroy and C. Noonan, *Producing British Television Drama*,
https://doi.org/10.1057/978-1-137-57875-4_4

PSB Drama and Cultural Representation

There is a dearth of critical literature that attends to the regional and national structure of contemporary UK television drama production. This is despite the fact that in the UK, place shapes the television sector in complex and often subtle ways. Our research tells us that this plays a profound role in shaping contemporary UK television drama both in terms of the on-screen creative representations that emerge and the structural organisation of drama's production.

Public service broadcasting is intrinsically bound to conceptions of place. Structurally, for example, the commercial PSB, ITV, was established by the Television Act 1954 as a service comprising several regional companies in an attempt to leverage value from local advertising, and in contrast to the centralised ethos of the BBC (see Johnson and Turnock 2005). Scotland continues to be served by a separate Channel 3 broadcaster, STV. While ITV's regional make-up reflects largely commercial realities, the BBC's commitment to the regions and nations is driven more by a public service agenda (see Harvey and Robins 1994) that is incorporated via the BBC's Charter and through the regulator, Ofcom. Despite the fact that the BBC's production systems are founded on a relationship between the main network and several regional and national services, this aspect of the BBC's production structure is frequently neglected by television scholars and is not widely understood by licence-fee payers. The BBC is a UK-wide broadcaster based in London which commissions and transmits content on what is termed the 'network'. However, it also has regional services across England (for example, BBC North West) and national services in Northern Ireland (BBC Northern Ireland), Wales (BBC Cymru Wales) and Scotland (BBC Scotland and the Gaelic service, BBC Alba). Compared with the BBC central 'network' operation, these services have modest budgets with which to make regional programming—Table 3.1 in the previous chapter outlines the different tariffs applied to 'network' and 'nations and regions' drama. These regional and national services are termed 'opt-outs', premised on the idea that the nations and regions are opting out of the central, mainstream UK service for the period of a specific programme's transmission. Indeed, this nomenclature signifies the BBC's historical view of itself as normatively London-based.

The political structures of the UK have, evolved considerably since the creation of both BBC and ITV. In particular, devolution presents a major challenge for the BBC as an institution premised on serving specifically British ideals. Devolution is the process whereby governmental powers held by the UK government in Westminster (London) were transferred to the different nations of the UK from 1997 onwards. Each of the three national governments in Northern Ireland, Scotland and Wales hold different policy-making powers, however none have powers over broadcasting policy.[1] This gives rise to peculiar anomalies. For example, powers over Welsh-language broadcasters remain based in Westminster (see McElroy et al. 2017). In contrast, business and culture are devolved to all three national governments, hence all three can enact measures geared to supporting their own screen sectors and attracting inward investment from global production companies.

As Cushion et al argue, while the BBC's 'instinct might be to address commonalities in the UK […] Understanding devolution requires […] more than an appreciation of administrative technicalities, but a stretching of our concept of nationhood to embrace not singularity but difference' (2009, 16). Following the 2016 Brexit referendum—which saw stark regional variations in UK voting patterns—there has been renewed attention on the substantial economic and cultural differences across the UK. This political focus on regional differences has impacted on broadcasting. Perhaps the best example of this is Channel 4's relocation process. In 2017, the UK government's Department for Digital, Culture, Media and Sport held a public consultation on how best to increase the regional impact of Channel 4. A year later, Channel 4 launched '4 All the UK', a UK-wide competition for cities to bid to become home to a new headquarters for the broadcaster outside London, alongside a competition to locate two new creative hubs, again outside London. A PSB established with the express purpose of serving minority interests and audiences, Channel 4 found itself having to respond to the political agenda of decentralising broadcasting from London. Channel 4's pitching guidance, 'A Call 4 All', states its aim to 'boost investment and jobs in the Nations and Regions' and to 'do even more to serve the whole of

---

[1] Since 2017, six English regions have 'combined authorities' and have had powers and budgets devolved from the UK central government with some of these also having directly elected city mayors (e.g. Greater Manchester). Combined authorities are devolved from central government assuming power for areas such as transport, housing, planning, skills and economic development, although their specific duties vary from area to area. To date, English voters have rejected English regional devolved governments.

the UK' (2018, 2). In late 2018, Leeds was awarded the new headquarters with smaller hubs in Bristol and Glasgow. In addition, Channel 4 promised to increase significantly their nations and regions content spend from the current quota of 35% to a voluntary target of 50%, a move that effectively pre-empted action by the communications regulator Ofcom to the same end. Regional production, and its regulation, testifies to how UK public service broadcasting is shaped by changing geopolitical realities, not just by evolving technologies or market shifts.

Driven by political will, Channel 4's move echoes the BBC's earlier nations and regions strategy, 'Beyond the M25: A BBC for all of the UK' (Bennett 2008).[2] It set a target for the BBC to achieve 50% of spend on 'Made Outside London' productions by 2016 and to source 17% of network productions from the nations. This target has been met but, as explored below, this is not without some gameplaying. A major element of the 'Beyond the M25' strategy was the creation of in-house production centres of excellence across the UK. Wales leads on drama production, which was largely the result of the success in making the relaunched *Doctor Who* (which we return to in the next chapter). Carving up of the UK into specialist production centres felt arbitrary to many and it demonstrates how 'BBC TV drama is a bit like an ecosystem where what happens in one part can affect what happens in another' (Cook 2015). Moreover, it led to quite convoluted actions in order to meet the new targets. For example, in 2011, the decision was taken to relocate the popular school drama *Waterloo Road* (2006–2015) from Rochdale in North West England to Greenock in Scotland. Relocating an existing drama to Scotland helped the BBC meet its targeted increase in network production from the nations. As Cameron Roach, executive producer at Shed Productions (who made the series for the BBC) explains, 'drama is a notoriously slow genre to develop, and so one option for fast-tracking volume of network hours in this genre was to move an existing network show' (Roach 2014, 184–185). This tactic came to be known by its critics as 'lift and shift', that is to lift a production from one location and shift it to another in order to meet regions and nations production quotas (Table 4.1).

This strategy means that while some regions and nations gain, others lose the economic benefit of having a returning series based locally.

---

[2] The M25 or London Orbital Motorway is a 117 mile motorway encircling almost all of Greater London.

Table 4.1 Current regional production quotas

		BBC	ITV	Channel 4	Channel 5
Production outside the M25	% of network programme hours	50%	35%	35%	10%
	% of production spend	50%	35%	35%	10%
Production in the Nations	% of network programme hours	England outside M25: 30% Scotland: 8% Wales: 4% (5% from 2020) Northern Ireland: 2% (3% from 2020)	N/A	3% (9% from 2020)	N/A
	% of production spend	England outside M25: 28% (30% from 2020) Scotland: 8% Wales: 5% Northern Ireland: 3%	N/A	3% (9% from 2020)	N/A

Source Ofcom licences for PSBs (Ofcom 2018a, 11)

Note BBC quotas apply to BBC television overall, while ITV, Channel 4 and Channel 5 quotas apply only to the main PSB channel

Wales for example, has benefitted from this strategy following the development of the BBC's state-of-the-art drama studios at Roath Lock in Cardiff in 2011 (see McElroy and Noonan 2016). Mainstream dramas based there include the long-running medical drama *Casualty* (1986–present) which was relocated from Bristol to the new studios in Cardiff. The creation of Roath Lock studios helped the BBC meet and exceed its target for network productions, with BBC Cymru Wales now producing dramas as varied as *Sherlock* (2010–2017), *War and Peace* (2016) and the Welsh-language soap opera, *Pobol y Cwm* which it makes for the Welsh-language broadcaster, S4C. The BBC also co-produces *Y Gwyll/Hinterland* (2013–present), *Craith/Hidden* (2018–present) and *Un Bore Mercher/Keeping Faith* (2017–present) with S4C. As argued elsewhere (McElroy and Noonan 2016), the strategic investment in Roath Lock, as part of a wider policy by the BBC of increasing network production in the nations, has contributed substantially to Wales' growing production base, helping it develop not only a national but an international reputation for high-end television drama production. This growth in global production and reputation is also discernible in new commercial entities such as Bad Wolf—makers of *A Discovery of Witches*

(2018–present) and *His Dark Materials* (2019)—which is led by former BBC Cymru Wales drama commissioner, Julie Gardner, and former BBC Head of Fiction, Jane Tranter, and which has been supported by substantial Welsh Government funding. Devolved governments have thus invested public funds in commercial productions as part of their own business policies (see Ramsey et al. 2019). Moreover, several of these dramas have been distributed by BBC Worldwide, testifying to the interwoven nature of global distribution flows and the enduring salience of national regulation on television drama production.

While the 'Beyond the M25' strategy met its targets for decentralising production, many regions and nations of the UK remain under-represented on screen. There is an important conceptual distinction to be drawn here between regional production (understood as the location where television is made), and regional representation (how regions and nations appear on screen). Many of the quotas and targets for diversifying production in the UK are targeted at the places in which productions are located, not at the way those places are represented or portrayed on screen. This matters because:

> The circulation of stories has historically been a crucial means of cultural identification, and of articulating and negotiating our understanding of others and ourselves. Since television affords a major means of everyday story-telling in the contemporary world, TV fictions, as produced and distributed locally, regionally, nationally and globally, afford sites of identification and resistance, sites of negotiation of our place in a fast-changing world. (Nelson 2007, 5)

Drama enjoys unique cultural significance but making Cardiff into the BBC's base for drama production did not in itself translate into more dramas appearing on screen which were set in or about Wales. As freelance television producer and researcher Angela Graham (2014) has noted, 'we cannot be complacent about the welcome success of network product. Although that benefits Wales in many important ways it is, more often than not, content which is not culturally specific to Wales. It could be made anywhere'. Indeed, recognition of concerns about on-screen representation has lead Ofcom to conduct an inquiry into the BBC's representation and portrayal of the UK (Ofcom 2018b). It notes that 'people want to see representation of the UK outside of its major cities, and especially London' (Ofcom 2018b, 4).

Table 4.2   Ofcom criteria for 'Made Outside London'

Criteria	Detail
(1) Production company must have a substantive business and production base in the UK outside the M25	A base will be taken to be substantive if it is the usual place of employment of executives managing the regional business, of senior personnel involved in the production in question, and of senior personnel involved in seeking programme commissions
(2) At least 70% of the production budget must be spent in the UK outside the M25	This excludes the cost of on-screen talent, archive material, sports rights, competition prize money and copyright costs
(3) At least 50% of the production talent (i.e. not on-screen talent) by cost must have their usual place of employment in the UK outside the M25	Freelancers without a usual place of employment outside the M25 count for this purpose if they live outside the M25

NB: To qualify as a regional production two of the three criteria must be met by a production

As we highlighted in Chapter 1, the example of the internationally acclaimed *Sherlock* is illustrative here. It is made by Hartswood Films, whose main office is in London, with the series shown on BBC One, the network's flagship channel. Yet it counts towards the BBC's target for network drama from the nations. This is because Hartswood Films' opened a second, dedicated nations and regions office in Cardiff in 2010 which meant that it could meet one of the 'Made Outside London' criteria set by Ofcom for qualification as a regional production (see Table 4.2: Ofcom criteria for 'Made Outside London'). Cardiff benefits from its ability to pass for a more expensive location (London) but, as Greg Elmer argues in the case of Canada, there are cultural and economic costs with being the 'stand-in actor' (2005, 431) for other national landscapes. As one of our Screening the Nation respondents observed, 'If it's filmed in Wales like *Doctor Who*, why stick up London signs? It's filmed in Cardiff!' (Male youth focus group member from South Wales Valleys, 2010).

There are many reasons why failing to represent all parts of the UK matters, but one of the most important reasons lies in the BBC's public purpose. The BBC is required 'to reflect, represent and serve the diverse communities of all of the United Kingdom's nations and regions and, in doing so, support the creative economy' (Royal Charter 2016, Cm 9365 6(1)). While production quotas are a powerful instrument for supporting the creative economy of the UK, they do not directly address the cultural requirement to reflect and represent diverse communities. The Charter continues:

The BBC should reflect the diversity of the United Kingdom both in its output and services. In doing so, the BBC should accurately and authentically represent and portray the lives of the people of the United Kingdom today, and raise awareness of the different cultures and alternative viewpoints that make up its society. It should ensure that it provides output and services that meet the needs of the United Kingdom's nations, regions and communities.

There is a genuine irony in the fact that the 'Beyond the M25' strategy coincided with a significant period of funding cuts that had a harsh impact on some of the national BBC services. For example, between 2008–2015 spend on English-language programme in Wales by the BBC and ITV combined fell from £39 million to £27 million (see McElroy et al. 2017). Paradoxically, Cardiff gained international recognition as a drama production centre at the very point when BBC Cymru Wales experienced its most severe funding cuts, which resulted in no drama series being commissioned for the opt-out service. Rather than delivering on the ethos of a service for all and representing all, this pattern of drama commissioning left Welsh life and Welsh audiences under-represented on screen while indigenous Welsh independent productions companies also experienced a dearth of new local commissions. This major creative deficit was acknowledged by Director General of the BBC, Tony Hall, when he said:

> English language programming from and for Wales has been in decline for almost a decade. ... It means, inevitably, that there are some aspects of national life in Wales that are not sufficiently captured by the BBC's own television services in Wales. (Hall 2014)

Significantly, Hall argued that news alone could not meet the obligation to represent the diversity of the UK. Drama has a substantial role to play as 'the vitality of any nation must surely rest on more than its journalism. One cannot fully realise a nation's creative potential or harness its diverse talents through the important, but narrow, prism of news' (ibid.). It took three years for Hall's speech to result in any significant action but in 2017 the BBC announced a package of investment in the nations, including £8.5 million for English-language programmes for Wales and £30 million to create a new BBC Scotland channel that launched in 2019.

One outcome of this investment in Wales was *Un Bore Mercher/Keeping Faith*, a drama co-production with S4C made by

Cardiff-based Vox Pictures shot back-to-back in English and in Welsh. The series was broadcast first in Welsh on S4C, the Welsh-language public service broadcaster, then in English in Wales on BBC One Wales before moving to iPlayer. It was subsequently transmitted on network television across the UK, the first contemporary example of a BBC Cymru Wales/S4C joint TV drama production having been shown on BBC One. This female-led thriller stars Eve Myles as Faith, a lawyer in a small Welsh town whose husband suddenly disappears. Despite receiving the highest audience for a non-network drama shown in Wales in more than 20 years, BBC executives in London decided against selecting *Un Bore Mercher/Keeping Faith* for the central network, choosing instead *Requiem* (2018), a ghostly drama set in Wales but made by Manchester-based production company New Pictures. Consequently, the only way non-Welsh audiences in the UK could find *Un Bore Mercher/Keeping Faith* was via iPlayer. This is exactly what viewers did, often with the encouragement of press reviewers such as Stuart Heritage (2018):

> Consider this a call to action. On Friday at 11 pm, Welsh series Keeping Faith will vanish from iPlayer. If you haven't seen it, you must do whatever you can to watch it while it's still available. Stay up all night. Call in sick. Ignore your children. Whatever it takes. You'll thank me for it.

With no supporting marketing campaign from the BBC in London, *Un Bore Mercher/Keeping Faith* nevertheless achieved record viewing figures for a non-network drama on BBC iPlayer via word of mouth recommendations, with more than 9.5 million downloads. In light of this phenomenal success, the BBC finally aired the series on the network, transmitting it on BBC One in summer 2018. A second series is in development at the time of writing.

Un Bore Mercher/Keeping Faith's success reveals several things about contemporary drama and its relationship to local production. Firstly, it demonstrates how central PSBs are to making original drama that can both represent the diversity of the UK and support the creative economy by commissioning from independent production companies in the nations. Conversely, when a broadcaster like the BBC fails to deliver on these public purposes and cynically navigates them by deploying 'lift and shift' strategies, it not only distorts the independent production sector, but it also loses the public support necessary to maintain the broadcaster's legitimacy. Secondly, the case of *Un Bore Mercher/Keeping Faith* testifies to the enduring tensions existing within the BBC's commissioning structure between a still highly centralised network centre in London on the one hand, and the modest commissioning budgets and limited autonomy of the nations and regions offices on the other. The success of *Un Bore Mercher/Keeping Faith* was a feather in the cap of BBC Cymru Wales and its drama commissioner, Nick Andrews, but time will tell whether this actually signals a more responsive and inclusive approach to commissioning drama beyond the M25. Thirdly, the successful co-production between BBC Cymru Wales and S4C on this production and others demonstrates the opportunities available to PSBs to collaborate successfully without losing their distinct identities or inhibiting their capacity to serve distinct audiences. And finally, what we see in *Un Bore Mercher/Keeping Faith*'s popularity is an increasing digital maturity among UK viewers who, when given the opportunity by broadcasters, will find dramas to love online even when schedulers and commissioners perceive no broad appeal for them.

The privileges enjoyed by the BBC come with socio-cultural responsibilities and a duty to produce content that has a wider cultural, and not just economic, purpose. Public service broadcasting and the drama it produces cannot be divorced from its cultural value. This is not unique to Britain. The Australian Special Broadcasting Service (SBS), for example, describes itself as 'a guardian of Australia's cultural and creative identity' committed to 'telling stories – stories that help Australians understand who we are, where we have come from and what we could become' (SBS 2018). Similarly, Stine Sand argues that Norwegian regional television productions are seen 'as cultural expressions of Norwegian culture and identity and therefore should represent the whole country and not just Oslo' (2017, 92). These fine-grained requirements have been long established for PSBs, in contrast to the modest regulatory frameworks now taking shape for global players such as Netflix, Amazon Prime, Youtube, Apple and Disney. Nonetheless, in Europe at least, there is a growing pressure to regulate the local content provision of video on demand and video streaming services. In October 2018 the European Parliament approved measures that require these services to dedicate at least 30% of their on-demand catalogues to local content. While Netflix has challenged such moves—both in Europe and Australia—the move towards regulation of global SVODs signals an increasing concern by regulators and governments with safeguarding both the economic and cultural value of local production.

PRODUCING PLACE ON SCREEN

Place is a significant element in the structural organisation of UK drama production, but it is also a profoundly meaningful component of creative production. Here we focus on how the representation of place, people and landscapes contribute to the cinematic qualities of contemporary television production as a public good. Many scholars and industry professionals argue that television drama has become an increasingly writerly medium, which begs the question of what role place plays in a writer's vision. In UK drama, one of the best examples of a writer whose work is known for its very strong sense of place is Sally Wainwright. Her credits include *At Home with the Braithwaites* (2002–2003), *Scott and Bailey* (2011–2016), *Unforgiven* (2009), *Last Tango in Halifax* (2012–2016), *Happy Valley* (2014–present) and *To Walk Invisible* (2016). Wainwright's writing marries specific landscapes and local vernacular with the overall narrative and character of individual series. Aesthetically, the creation of a sense of place significantly enriches the dramatic narrative, providing a great deal more than just a backdrop to the action. Discussing her crime drama, *Unforgiven*, for example, Wainwright describes how:

> The landscape was another character almost and the house was another character. Right from early on we were thinking in those terms of that bleak but beautiful landscape where the farm was and the urban landscape of Halifax as well, being intrinsic to the mood of it and the feel and style of it. (Screen Yorkshire 2009)

Wainwright is one of relatively few UK writers who enjoys sufficient power to be able to deliver so consistently on her own vision:

> I wrote it [*Unforgiven*] very definitely set in Yorkshire. There was no reason to shoot it anywhere else … I tend to write in my own voice and my own vernacular which is West Yorkshire. It fitted that landscape, it fitted the mood of that landscape. (Screen Yorkshire 2009)

Wainwright's long-standing working relationship with Salford-based Red Productions and with producer Karen Lewis has enabled her to maintain significant control of her script and a consistent presence on set that few writers enjoy. Describing the process of location scouting for *Unforgiven*, Wainwright reveals how integral she is as a writer to a production:

I went out with Karen who produced it and Brett who's the production manager and Brett said, 'Show me where you set it, show me what you've got in mind.' So, we just drove round. The farmhouse where I used to visit when I was little because my friend lived there and so they knocked on the door and asked if they could use it and they were fine. A lot of places, well a number of them, were just places I knew. (Screen Yorkshire 2009)

As a television writer, Wainwright is alert to the visual and aural elements of her narrative and is an active presence on set. This is discernible in how her dramas often entail the photographic composition of character in a specific locale, enriching both the viewer's appreciation of the complexity of that character while also embedding them and their crime(s) within the landscape itself. This technique is also one way in which television is cinematic, using lingering establishing shots and contrasting characters against carefully composed landscapes. To situate a character within a specific landscape is also to signify the value of an entire place, its histories, practices, and human geography. This is what lends place such potency. As Wainwright explains:

[T]here were some brilliant images [in *Unforgiven*] like Ruth standing on the wall and it wasn't all idyllic or soft, but it was dramatic and beautiful but bleak as well. I think it was a fantastic mixture of what that part of the world is – very beautiful but very harsh as well. (ibid.)

Wainwright's signature is shaped by this intimacy and feeling for a specific part of the world; it is integral to her work's authenticity and its appeal to viewers and critics alike. Rather than limiting the appeal of her drama to Yorkshire viewers, Wainwright regards this sense of place as integral to the identity of her writing: 'I'm sure you could set that story anywhere, it's a universal story, but I wanted to set it in West Yorkshire, yes *definitely*' (ibid.). Here, we can see the value of a television writer being able to access and work with a northern production team over a period of time, committing to a specific landscape and its vernacular to develop a story from within that everyday world. Rather than reducing its appeal, the creative use of place allows drama to expand its horizons and signify multiple aesthetic, cultural and psychological meanings.

In our earlier research, *Screening the Nation* (Blandford et al. 2010), we found evidence of how important place is to audiences' enjoyment of drama. One of our younger focus groups in the South Wales Valleys, for example, talked appreciatively of how '*Torchwood* represents the Cardiff we know' and 'it's almost like I can get a sense of heritage from *Doctor Who* and *Torchwood* being filmed in Cardiff. It's like, "Yes! I'm in the place with the aliens!"'. Representing a recognisable place on screen can help legitimise the cultural and historical value of that place for viewers even when working outside realist fictional forms. By the same token, however, the failure to acknowledge place is a powerful form of delegitimation and one which audiences contested in our original *Screening the Nation* research:

> If you watch *Torchwood* or *Doctor Who* it only shows the location. It doesn't show the culture and it doesn't show the people properly. (Welsh-speaking focus group member from North Wales 2010)

Place is a far richer concept than location alone and scholars are increasingly recognising that its value to television drama extends far beyond its role as a backdrop (see Toft Hansen and Waade 2017; Waade 2011). Place may play a psychological and symbolic role in a dramatic narrative as well as a cultural and social one. In the UK, regional crime drama has a long-standing history in both literary and televisual form. This form provides PSBs with a ready route into locating popular drama in diverse topographies across the UK. Examples include *Rebus* (2000–2004), the STV series based on Ian Rankin's Edinburgh crime novels, *DCI Banks* (2010–present) based on Peter Robinson's Yorkshire police detective, and *Vera* (2011–present) based on Ann Cleeves' novels set in a fictional Northumberland and City police force. Christopher Bigsby organises his examination of US television drama through the locations in which series such as *The Sopranos* (1999–2007) and *Friday Night Lights* (2006–2011) are set. In these series, 'authenticity of character and social circumstance … depended on a specific environment' meaning not only the social observation of reality but the meaningful contrast between 'suburban tranquillity and a downmarket seediness' (2013, 16). Jonathan Nichols-Pethick, meanwhile, points to the use of urban cityscapes in US series *The Wire* (2002–2008) in order 'to construct a gritty narrative of Baltimore crime that engages what we might call the sociological imagination of crime and corruption in urban America' (2012, 173).

In a drama such as ITV's *Broadchurch* (2013–2017), for example, the fictional seaside town of Broadchurch operated metonymically, representing small town life. More than this, its Dorset coast location enabled dramatic and stunning shots of its limestone cliffs—the excess of which both symbolises and amplifies the melodrama of the violent and shocking crime committed in the town. The repeated shots of the cliffs act visually and thematically as a leitmotif of a town on the edge. Accomplishing this effect routinely and within budget requires cinematographic skills, and new technological capabilities. As Helen Wheatley (2011) has argued, spectacular landscapes on screen are enhanced by technological developments such as high-definition (HD) filming. This also contributes to the international popularity of series such as *Downton Abbey* (2010–2015) and *The Crown* (2016–present) which shoot quintessentially English locations such as stately homes that look alluringly exotic to many foreign viewers and which come to represent 'Brand Britain' (Groskop 2014). As we discuss in Chapter 6, shooting on location in turn helps fuel television tourism to places such as Highclere Castle, the real-life *Downton Abbey*.

Linguistic Cultures and TV Drama

Language is one of the most powerful ways in which a sense of place can be created aurally on screen. As Novrup Redvall argues in a Danish context, it is also 'a crucial part of a public service obligation to represent a variety of national stories in the native language on the small screen' (2013, 39). S4C has commissioned a series of crime dramas including *Y Gwyll/Hinterland, Craith/Hidden* and *Un Bore Mercher/Keeping Faith* that are shot back-to-back by first shooting a scene in Welsh and then shooting the exact same scene in English using actors (but not necessarily all crew) who speak both languages. The creation of a credible on-screen world requires a production team to consider whether and how to capture the linguistic realities of the place where the narrative is set. Frequently, characteristics of everyday speech are filtered to conform to existing dramatic conventions. One of these conventions is the monolingual nature of television drama in which all characters speak the same language all the time unless there is an overt narrative reason that mandates they do otherwise (for example, a trip abroad). While code-switching—moving between languages—is a natural feature of bilingual speech patterns, few TV dramas represent this reality on screen. Yet as Catrin Lewis Defis, producer of S4C's bilingual police series *Bang* (2017) explains, 'I move between speaking Welsh to Welsh-speaking friends and English to English-speaking friends almost within the same paragraph' (Lewis Defis cited in Walford 2017). Set in Port Talbot, a predominantly English-speaking industrial town in South Wales, *Bang* consciously creates a bilingual storyworld that challenges the monolingualism of British TV drama. Actor Jacob Ifan, the series' male lead, explained how Roger Williams' script included code-switching in a manner that 'is actually reflective of how people do exist and speak in Wales' (cited in Walford 2017).

This aural authenticity is integral to a cultural vision of drama's purpose; as Ifan put it: 'In drama, I always feel that the duty of the production is to reflect the societies that we live in' (ibid.). Moreover, when drama creates a bilingual sense of place, it often challenges wider social politics. Writing about US series such as *Jane the Virgin* (2014–present) and *Fresh off the Boat* (2015–present), Alexis Gunderson (2018) points to how these broadcast network shows allow mainstream American audiences to engage with 'the eminently relatable lives of bilingual families whose specific experiences with immigration … are central to many of the biggest political fights we are facing'. Drama's capacity to immerse viewers in lives not their own is enhanced when it offers audiences greater space for their own engagement; as Ifan puts it 'we need to trust audiences because we're plenty used to doing that with TV shows now: programmes such as *The Bridge* or *Narcos* where people are far more open to subtitles and the like' (cited in Walford 2017).

An appreciation of place on screen is shaped by audiences' exposure to transnational content. Historically, the UK had been regarded as an exceptionally difficult territory into which to export non-English language content (see Jensen and Waade 2013). This changed in 2006 when BBC Four made a strategic investment in imported European drama beginning with the French crime series *Spiral/Engrenages* (2005–present) as part of its branding strategy, itself a consequence of having too small a budget to commission many original dramas (see McCabe 2016). Meanwhile, in Denmark and Sweden PSBs had already developed a new strategic vision for drama production which yielded successful exports such as *Wallander* (2008–2016), *The Killing* (2011–2014), *Bron/Broen/The Bridge* (2011–2018) and *Borgen* (2010–2013) (see Aveyard et al. 2016). It is the success of imported European drama which the producers of Welsh-language drama credit for their success with British broadcasters.

Beautifully shot by award-winning cinematographers Hubert Taczanowski and Richard Stoddard, *Y Gwyll/Hinterland* is set in the western coastal town of Aberystwyth and revolves around DCI Tom Mathias (Richard Harrington) who returns to Wales following a career

in metropolitan London. A striking feature of the series in all its itera-
tions is the care taken visually and aurally to create a compelling sense of
place. The cinematic pace of filming enhances the series' sense of con-
cealed crimes being slowly revealed in a close-knit community. Shots
are slow and lingering, and the lighting allows for shadow and texture,
capturing both the seascape and isolated rural inland mountains and
hamlets around the town. As press reviewer Ceri Radford (2014) noted:

> The scenery colluded in the drama from the offset. Whether it was wind-
> blown blocks of bright primary colours – green cliffs, blue sea – or the
> damp, drizzle-soaked greys and ochres of tangled trees, slippery moss and
> Victorian stone, there was a sense of capriciousness and subtle menace
> woven right through the production.

The series exploits Mathias' outsider status in Aberystwyth, as do many
crime dramas that place their detective at a slant to the communities
they police. His outsider status is captured visually, for instance, when
he is shot running solo along the dramatic Ceredigion cliffs to his sham-
bolic old caravan on the edge, a visual leitmotif that *Y Gwyll/Hinterland*
shares with *Broadchurch*, Britain's island coastline providing a rich natural resource for cinematographers. But Mathias is also positioned as an
outsider to this community by the use of language.

This creative route is exploited most effectively in the bilingual version of *Hinterland* which was transmitted on BBC Cymru Wales, as
opposed to either the Welsh-language version *Y Gwyll* which was transmitted on S4C or the English-language version transmitted on BBC
Four across the UK. In the bilingual version, code-switching is used
to signify the stronger, historical and personal bonds which Mathias'
side-kick, DI Mared Rhys (Mali Harries), enjoys both with her fellow
police officers and also with the witnesses and suspects who they investigate. Frequently, Mared speaks in English with Mathias in police pre-
cinct scenes only to switch to Welsh when they encounter local people
in the local community where she has lived most of her life. This use
of code-switching enriches the characterisation of Mared while the representation of a bilingual environment dramatises the quotidian practice
of Welsh speakers in changing to English when working with non-Welsh
speakers such as Mathias. Creatively, it normalises bilingualism as a characteristic of the place and its people while also demonstrating the limits

to Mathias' knowledge and the necessity for collaboration between the two detectives, another hallmark of the investigative genre.

Here then we can see how the popular, transnational genre of crime is developed within a specific set of cultural, linguistic and commissioning contexts to allow for creative distinction and a specific sense of place (Weissmann 2018). Moreover, the different versions of *Y Gwyll/Hinterland* themselves testify to the mutability of place and its subtly different resonance for each audience and channel. Place is not one thing in the series, nor are its meanings fixed. In making *Y Gwyll*, for example, series co-producer Ed Talfan recounted how the priority was to create a credible linguistic universe in order that both the original broadcaster, S4C, and the Welsh-speaking audience be convinced by the series' storyworld:

> We pitched the show to them [S4C] that would have a keen sense of place, set in Aberystwyth. We were keen to depict a part of Wales that was very rarely seen on screen, keen to go to a place that had real identity and also to go to a place where, from S4C's point of view, a Welsh-language cop show would ring true. (Interview with *Hinterland* series co-producer and co-creator Ed Talfan 2015)

Talfan's logic is impeccable for a Welsh-speaking audience already familiar with the country's linguistic map. However, the role of the Welsh language in creating the series' sense of place was also regarded positively by distributors all3Media and subsequently by international buyers at trade fairs. *Y Gwyll/Hinterland* was screened at the 2013 MIPCOM[3] by all3Media alongside S4C and the series' producers:

> On this journey, since we have started, they have kind of realised that there's a clamour and interest and genuine curiosity in the Welsh language … when the Danes came last week … they were intrigued. We showed them four minutes in Welsh and then we showed them the screening, and half the questions everywhere, in every Q&A, has been about the Welsh and English issue, which we didn't expect. Nor did S4C expect, they certainly didn't expect such curiosity and warmth from all3Media. (Interview with *Hinterland* series co-producer and co-creator Ed Thomas 2015)

---

[3] MIPCOM is the annual global television trade fair held each October in Cannes, France. It brings together the acquisition and distribution wings of television production. Other major fairs include NATPE (National Association of Television Program Executives), held in the US every winter, and the LA Screenings held in Los Angeles each May/June.

Sellers at television trade fairs must hook international buyers often with just a single episode and a clear pitch that offers a credible, distinctive product that buyers can feel confident will find an audience and enhance their own channel brand (Harrington and Bielby 2005). As Havens argues, trade fairs are as much cultural as commercial spaces. They demand a range of interpersonal skills including cultivating relationships with distributors 'establishing and renewing relationships with buyers, gathering information about the industry and competitors, creating awareness of new products, and generating or maintaining corporate images' (2003, 21). As discussed in the previous chapter, distributors are vital actors in these cultural encounters as they bridge local drama production and global acquisition markets. For producers from lesser-known territories, selling internationally requires substantial cultural translation work and support. The combination of the internationally popular crime drama genre and the quirky linguistic combination of global English and a niche Welsh-speaking setting seems to have been vital to the series' appeal to international buyers.

The discourses employed by the producers in their selling and marketing of the series, together with those employed in press coverage, reveal how complex the creation of a sense of place is when seeking to situate television drama in a televisual landscape. The creators of *Y Gwyll/Hinterland* were familiar with the necessity of explaining and translating Wales to those who know nothing about the country or its language. This translational mindset is a common characteristic of small nations and of minority-language speakers, something which frequently emerged in the collaborative workshops that formed the backbone of our 'Television Production in Small Nations' network. In writing about cinema in small nations, one of our participants, Mette Hjort, argues for an appreciation of what she terms 'affinitive transnationalism', that is 'cross-border solidarities and collaborative endeavours that find a starting point in a reciprocal sense of affinity' (Hjort 2011). Rhetorically at least, the success of subtitled 'Nordic noir' provides a discursive space through which Welsh-language and bilingual drama may find a place in the international drama marketplace. As executive producer Ed Thomas put it in interview with us, 'I think we owe it to the confidence of the Scandis rather than anything that's changed within the M25 … But the very fact that those As and Bs are looking at Welsh in the same way they look at Danish is a plus'. The popularity of Nordic Noir on niche channel, BBC Four aimed at an educated, older middle-class audience (the As and Bs to which Thomas refers) is more profoundly influential in Thomas' view than the Beyond London Strategy which, he implies, has done little to change the deeper mindset of the BBC. Policy targets are a significant regulatory instrument, but market success and good ratings appear to have greatest purchase on changing minds in London.

New digital distributions systems have the potential to make a wider, richer array of geographical places available to viewers. The architecture of digital platforms—what they make visible and readily accessible—holds genuine opportunities to build audiences for drama from beyond the dominant, mainstream centres of television production. Herein lies a powerful tension that broadcasters are still negotiating, between cleaving ever more tightly to proven gatekeeping mechanisms on the one hand, and genuinely liberating content (and viewers) into a more dynamic digital landscape on the other. These examples illustrate some of the complexities and rewards for television drama production as it engages with place. In the competitive landscape of television, place is a marker of distinction whether it be as an appealing location for filming, delivering on its social responsibilities, or enhancing the narrative authenticity of drama. In the next chapter we will turn our attention to those who inhabit the places of production—the workers.

REFERENCES

Aveyard, Karina, Pia Majbritt Jensen and Albert Moran. *New Patterns in Global Television Formats*. Bristol: Intellect Books, 2016.

Bennett, Jana. 'Beyond the M25: A BBC for All of the UK'. Speech to the Royal Television Society, 15 October 2008. Accessed 8 November 2018. http://www.bbc.co.uk/pressoffice/speeches/stories/bennett_beyond_m25.shtml.

Bigsby, Christopher. *Viewing America: Twenty-First Century Television Drama*. Cambridge: Cambridge University Press, 2013.

Blandford, Steve, Stephen Lacey, Ruth McElroy and Rebecca Williams. 'Screening the Nation: Wales and Landmark Television'. Report for the BBC Trust/Audience Council Wales, 2010. http://culture.research.southwales.ac.uk/screeningthenation/.

Channel 4. 'A Call 4 All. Pitch Process'. Accessed 1 July 2018. http://www.channel4.com/media/documents/press/news/4+All+the+UK+-+Pitch+brochure_DIGITAL+FINAL.pdf.

Cook, John. 'Is Doctor Who Exterminating BBC Drama Round the UK?' *The Conversation*, 18 September 2015. Accessed 24 March 2019. https://theconversation.com/is-doctor-who-exterminating-bbc-drama-around-the-uk-47796.

Cushion, Stephen, Justin Lewis and Christopher Groves. 'Prioritizing Hand-Shaking Over Policy-Making: A Study of How the 2007 Devolved Elections Was Reported on BBC UK Network Coverage'. *Cyfrwng: Media Wales Journal* 6 (2009): 7–32.

Elmer, Greg and Mike Gasher. *Contracting Out Hollywood: Runaway Productions and Foreign Location Shooting.* Lanham: Rowman and Littlefield, 2005.

Graham, Angela. 'What Tony Said—What Wales Replied'. *Click on Wales*, 18 May 2014. Accessed 28 July 2014. http://www.clickonwales.org/2014/05/what-tony-said-what-wales-replied/.

Groskop, Viv. 'Downton Abbey's Class Nostalgia Is Another Toxic British Export'. *The Guardian*, 17 September 2014. Accessed 5 September 2018. https://www.theguardian.com/commentisfree/2014/sep/17/downton-abbey-nostalgia-british-export-stereotypes.

Gunderson, Alexis. 'The Rise of Bilingual Families on Broadcast Television'. *Paste Magazine*, 28 February 2018. Accessed 1 July 2018. https://www.pastemagazine.com/articles/2018/02/the-rise-of-bilingual-families-on-broadcast-televi.html.

Hall, Tony. 'Speech at the National Assembly for Wales Reception'. 1 April 2014. Accessed 25 July 2014. http://www.bbc.co.uk/mediacentre/speeches/2014/dg-wales.

Harrington, Lee and Denise Bielby. 'Flow, Home and Media Pleasures'. *The Journal of Popular Culture* 38, 5 (2005): 834–854.

Harvey, Sylvia and Kevin Robins. 'Voices and Places: The BBC and Regional Policy'. *The Political Quarterly* 65, 1 (1994): 39–52.

Havens, Timothy J. 'On Exhibiting Global Television: The Business and Cultural Functions of Global Television Fairs'. *Journal of Broadcasting & Electronic Media* 47, 1 (2003): 18–35.

Heritage, Stuart. 'Keeping Faith Is About to Vanish from iPlayer'. *iNews*, 2 May 2018. Accessed 8 November 2018. https://inews.co.uk/culture/television/keeping-faith-is-about-to-vanish-from-iplayer/.

Hjort, Mette. 'Small Cinemas: How They Thrive and Why They Matter'. *Mediascapes*, Winter 2011. Accessed 8 November 2018. http://www.tft.ucla.edu/mediascape/Winter2011_SmallCinemas.html.

Jensen, Pia and Anne Marit Waade. 'Nordic Noir Challenging the "Language of Advantage": Setting, Light and Language as Production Values in Danish Television Series'. *Journal of Popular Television* 1, 2 (2013): 259–265.

Johnson, Catherine and Rob Turnock (eds). *ITV Cultures: Independent Television Over 50 Years.* Maidenhead: Open University Press, 2005.

McCabe, Janet. 'Wallander at the BBC: Trading Fiction, Producing Culture and UK Public Service Broadcasting in the Contemporary Age'. In *New Patterns in Global Television Formats*, edited by Karina Aveyard, Pia Majbritt Jensen and Albert Moran, 171–186. Bristol: Intellect Books, 2016.

McElroy, Ruth and Caitriona Noonan. 'Television Drama Production in Small Nations: Mobilities in a Changing Ecology'. *Journal of Popular Television* 4, 1 (2016): 109–127.

McElroy, Ruth with Christina Papagiannouli and Hywel Wiliam. 'Broadcasting After Devolution: Policy and Critique in the Welsh Media Landscape 2008–2015'. *International Journal of Cultural Policy*, 2017. https://doi.org/10.1 080/10286632.2016.1268133v.

Nelson, Robin. *State of Play. Contemporary "High-End" TV Drama*. Manchester: Manchester University Press, 2007.

Nichols-Pethick, Jonathan. *TV Cops: The Contemporary American Television Police Drama*. New York: Routledge, 2012.

Ofcom (a). 'Review of Regional TV Production and Programming Guidance: Call for Evidence'. 26 May 2018. Accessed 11 October 2018. https://www.ofcom.org.uk/__data/assets/pdf_file/0013/112315/call-evidence-regional-production-review.pdf.

Ofcom (b). 'Representation and Portrayal on BBC Television a Thematic Review'. 25 October 2018. Accessed 30 October 2018. https://www.ofcom.org.uk/__data/assets/pdf_file/0022/124078/report-bbc-representation-portrayal.pdf.

Radford, Ceri. 'Hinterland BBC Four Review: "a Corker"'. *The Telegraph*, 28 April 2014. Accessed 1 July 2018. https://www.telegraph.co.uk/culture/tvandradio/tv-and-radio-reviews/10793152/Hinterland-BBC-Four-review-a-corker.html.

Ramsey, Phil, Steve Baker and Robert Porter. 'Screen Production "On the Biggest Set in the World": Northern Ireland Screen and the Case of *Game of Thrones*'. *Media, Culture and Society*, 2019. https://doi.org/10.1177/0163443719831597.

Redvall, Eva Novrup. *Writing and Producing Television Draa in Denmark: From The Kingdom to The Killing*. Basingstoke: Palgrave Macmillan, 2013.

Roach, Cameron. 'Moving Waterloo Road from Rochdale to Greenock: Exploring a Sense of Place in Drama Series'. In *British Television Drama: Past, Present and Future*, edited by Jonathan Bignell and Stephen Lacey, 2nd edition, 184–190. Basingstoke: Palgrave Macmillan, 2014.

Royal Charter for the Continuance of the British Broadcasting Corporation 2016 (Cm 9365).

Sand, Stine. 'Different Places, Different Stories? The Importance of Place in Regional Film and Television Production'. In *Building Sustainable and Successful Film and Television Businesses: A Cross-National Perspective*, edited by Eva Bakøy, Roel Puijk and Andrew Spicer, 89–106. Bristol: Intellect, 2017.

SBS. 'What SBS Tells Me About Australia'. SBS. Accessed 11 October 2018. https://www.sbs.com.au/article/107831/what-sbs-tells-me-about-australia.

Screen Yorkshire. 'Writer Sally Wainwright on ITVs Hit Drama Unforgiven'. 9 March 2009. Accessed 8 November 2018. https://www.youtube.com/watch?v=1O5qyXJfy9c.

Toft Hansen, Kim and Anne Marit Waade. *Locating Nordic Noir. From Beck to The Bridge*. Cham, Switzerland: Palgrave Macmillan, 2017.

Waade, Anne Marit. 'Crime Scenes: Conceptualizing Ystad as a Location in the Swedish and the British Wallander TV Crime Series'. *Northern Lights: Film & Media Studies Yearbook* 9 (2011): 9–25.

Walford, Jessica. 'How a New Welsh TV Drama Wants to Replicate the Success of Scandinavian Show The Killing'. *Wales Online*, 16 September 2017. Accessed 5 September 2018. https://www.walesonline.co.uk/news/wales-news/how-new-welsh-tv-drama-13621547.

Weissmann, Elke. 'Local, National, Transnational: *Y Gwyll/Hinterland* as Crime of/for All Places'. In *European Television Crime Drama and Beyond*, edited by Kim Toft Hansen, Steven Peacock and Sue Turnbull, 119–137. Cham, Switzerland: Palgrave Macmillan, 2018.

Wheatley, Helen. 'Beautiful Images in Spectacular Clarity: Spectacular Television, Landscape Programming and the Question of (Tele)Visual Pleasure'. *Screen* 52, 2 (2011): 233–248.

Filmography

A Discovery of Witches (Bad Wolf 2018–present).

At Home with the Braithwaites (Yorkshire TV (YTV) 2002–2003).

Bang (Joio 2017).

Borgen (DR Fiktion 2010–2013).

Broadchurch (Kudos Film and Television, Imaginary Friends, ITV—Independent Television 2013–2017).

Bron/Broen/The Bridge (Filmlance International AB, Nimbus Film Productions 2011–2018).

Craith/Hidden (Severn Screen 2018–present).

Crown, The (Left Bank Pictures/Sony Pictures Television Production UK 2016–present).

DCI Banks (Left Bank Pictures/ITV—Independent Television 2010–present).

Doctor Who (BBC Wales 2005–present).

Downton Abbey (Carnival Films/ITV Studios 2010–2015).

Fresh off the Boat (Fierce Baby Productions/The Detective Agency/20th Century Fox Television 2015–present).

Friday Night Lights (Imagine Television/Film 44/NBC Universal Television/Universal Media Studios 2006–2011).

Happy Valley (Red Production 2014–present).

His Dark Materials (Bad Wolf/British Broadcasting Corporation/New Line Cinema/Scholastic 2019).

Jane the Virgin (Poppy Productions/RCTV/Electus/CBS Television Studios/Warner Bros. Television 2014–present).

Killing, The (DR/ZDF Enterprises 2011–2014).

Last Tango in Halifax (Red Production Company/British Broadcasting Corporation 2012–2016).

Pobol y Cwm (BBC Wales 1974–present).

Scott and Bailey (Red Production Company/Ingenious Broadcasting/Veredus Productions/Ipomen Productions 2011–2016).

Sherlock (Hartswood Films 2010–present).

Sopranos, The (Home Box Office/Brillstein Entertainment Partners/The Park Entertainment 1999–2007).

Spiral/Engrenages (Canal+/Son et Lumiére 2005–present).

To Walk Invisible (British Broadcasting Corporation/Public Broadcasting Service/Universum Film 2016).

Torchwood (BBC Wales/Canadian Broadcasting Company/BBC Worldwide Productions 2006–2011).

Un Bore Mercher/Keeping Faith (Vox Pictures/Acorn Media Enterprises 2017–present).

Unforgiven (Red Production Company 2009).

Wallander (Zodiak Entertainment/ARD Degeto Film/BBC Scotland/Film I Skane/Left Bank Pictures/TV4/WGBH/Yellow Bird 2008–2016).

War and Peace (BBC Cymru Wales/BBC Worldwide/Lookout Point 2016).

Waterloo Road (Shed Productions/British Broadcasting Corporation 2006–2015).

Wire, The (Blown Deadline Productions/Home Box Office 2002–2008).

Y Gwyll/Hinterland (Fiction Factory 2015–present).

CHAPTER 5

Building a Sustainable Labour Force

Abstract This chapter provides an empirically grounded analysis of the labour processes from which TV drama emerges. Few scholarly accounts of television drama attend to the occupational experiences of those who bring drama to our television screens, especially those generally referred to as 'the crew'. This chapter advances drama scholarship by analysing its distinct forms of labour and the tensions that emerge when seeking to create an agile, skilled and diverse workforce. It argues for more critical attention to the precarious conditions experienced by production crew resulting from the increasing internationalisation and deregulation of the TV industry. This analysis is grounded in substantive empirical findings, giving voice to the workers and decision-makers involved in the BBC's Roath Lock drama studios, a major strategic investment in TV drama labour force.

Keywords Television labour · Skills · Crew · Talent · BBC · Studios · *Doctor Who*

One element which distinguishes drama from other forms of television production is the sheer volume of human creativity and labour that needs to be harnessed within a single project. A series like *Doctor Who* (2005–present) brings together the creative and logistical talents of hundreds of highly skilled television workers who labour intensely to bring the Doctor's adventures to our screens. Yet, few academic discussions

© The Author(s) 2019   97
R. McElroy and C. Noonan, *Producing British Television Drama*,
https://doi.org/10.1057/978-1-137-57875-4_5

of television drama give sustained attention to the diverse roles needed to produce the shows so valued by industry and viewers, and even less attention to the economic, political and cultural challenges in cultivating and sustaining these roles and the people who inhabit them. With the exception of writers and showrunners or producers (see, for example Blandford 2013; Johnson 2013; Pateman 2018), television drama scholarship has largely neglected the labour involved in commissioning (discussed in Chapter 3) or the specific working conditions of those collectively known as 'the crew'.

Although often framed as such TV labour is neither singular nor homogenous (Caldwell 2008). In the production of television drama, there tends to be much complexity and exchange as workers move between genres and companies. Television drama also competes directly with other sectors, such as film and theatre, for its workforce. This chapter argues that drama production engages distinct forms of creative labour and that specific structural conditions emerge from this context. It begins by attending to the ways in which the drama labour force has evolved in light of the changing ecology of production, especially the internationalisation of production, the mobility of content and the deregulation of the sector. It points to the precarious conditions experienced by production crews and how current policy formations often marginalise these workers. Critical attention to the different experiences of workers within the production of television drama allows us to connect these concerns to wider questions about the nature of creative labour in a digital economy. Finally, we give voice to the workers and decision-makers involved in the BBC's Roath Lock drama studios in Cardiff. This case study examines some of the conditions, elements and interventions needed to build a sustainable television drama labour force.

Labour in TV Drama Production

The television industry is a sizeable employer in the UK's creative economy. In 2015 there were nearly 59,000 workers active in television production (Creative Skillset 2016).[1] These workers occupied roles across

---

[1] In 2018 Creative Skillset rebranded to ScreenSkills and merged with not-for-profit training organisation The Indie Training Fund. It also replaced its workforce survey with a quarterly Skills Forecasting Service. The survey published in 2016 is their last cross-sectoral census at the time of writing.

public broadcasting, satellite, cable companies and independent production companies, with a further 18,650 involved in VFX and post-production (ibid.). The *Creative Media Workforce Survey* (Creative Skillset 2015) indicates that 28% of those working in television reported working in drama production in the previous 12 months (approximately 15,000 workers), with 18% working on high-end drama (that is, drama costing over £1 million per broadcast hour to produce). The centrality of public service broadcasters to the television drama ecology is again evident in the opportunities for work with drama workers more likely to have worked for these broadcasters.

If we distil the figures from the survey further, we can see that the TV drama workforce comprises more women (56%) than men (44%), which is very similar to the overall TV workforce, and there is a slightly greater proportion of under-35s working within drama production. This is a highly educated workforce, with 71% having a degree. Overall, at the time of writing the television labour market is buoyed by a successful tax relief mechanism, a weak pound and rising demand for labour from new players (Creative Skillset 2017)—apparently, 'It's never been so good' (ibid., 8) to work in high-end television drama.

As discussed in earlier chapters, high-end drama presents an attractive proposition for both the industry and policy-makers who use it to enhance distinctiveness and to contribute to domestic and international agendas. The television industry regards employment within drama production as 'good work' and it is an attractive destination for workers attracted by the prospect of working on projects of scale. The scale of production can often mean more stable contracts, especially where production is more predictable such as within a returning or continuing series. Furthermore, the professional prestige of drama also bestows occupational value for many television workers. Drama is a form where you can build your reputation—an essential strategic currency in this labour market.

Roles such as commissioner and channel controller (discussed in Chapter 3) have grown in prominence and power since the 1990s as a result of increased marketisation within the television industry. Increasingly, these decision-makers oversee the provision of content, initiating and aligning projects with wider channel or organisational strategy, thereby moving 'fluently between the business and editorial aspects of their role' (Preston 2003) as they attempt to develop their own creative reputation. As this interviewee in our research acknowledges:

When you have a new commissioner they want their own new staff. They don't want just to be a caretaker or curator of somebody else's legacy. There are politics always involved in these things. … It's a creative job being a commissioner and you don't want to tie up all your investment in things that aren't putting your stamp on it. (Interview with Head of BBC Cymru Wales 2013)

Commissioners and channel controllers are often the public 'face' of an organisation's strategy and find themselves on a circuit of industry talks and panels discussing the genre and/or institution they represent. However, they are also often the subject of criticism because of their singular power, the homogeneity of their background and their tendency to cluster together in major production hubs such as London and Los Angeles. This often makes it difficult for suppliers outside of these identity groups and locales to gain access and build professional relationships meaning that location can be a barrier to greater workforce diversity (CAMEo 2018). As discussed in the previous chapter, this has implications for the range of stories and places seen on screen (see Spicer and Presence 2017; McElroy and Noonan 2016).

The most visible form of labour within television drama is creative authorship. In television drama this tends to be associated with scriptwriters, producers and actors, thereby differentiating television from film which is often regarded as a director's medium (Newcomb and Alley 1983). In technical terms this cohort is often termed 'the talent' or 'above the line' labour, and there is substantial value attached to their work.[2] The work produced by 'the talent' is often regarded as intrinsic and person-specific (Boyle 2018) and many drama productions are characterised by a distinct single vision, as the success of 'Nordic noir' illustrates (Jensen and Waade 2013; Redvall 2013). However, this overlooks the fact that complex forms of collaborative work are required for television production (Mann 2009).

Architects of the golden age of television drama include Sally Wainwright, Russell T. Davies, Peter Kosminsky, Steven Moffat, Jane

---

[2] In standard film budgeting and accountancy, a distinction (a 'line') is drawn between *above-the-line* and *below-the-line* costs. Costs/roles which are 'above the line' include the screenwriter, producer, director and actors, and are generally regarded as persons who need to be in place before a project can begin. On the other hand, 'below the line' refers to the other diverse (and often invisible) roles associated with production.

Campion, Shonda Rhimes, Dick Wolf, Jerry Bruckheimer, David E. Kelley, to name but a select few. Many of these will have learned and developed their craft initially as writers and will continue to function as writers alongside assuming additional creative and production roles. In contrast to the invisibility of much television labour, many of these will be household names. As Perren and Schatz argue:

> The ascendance of both "cult" and "quality" television—along with the expanded means by which creatives can interact directly with viewers and the networks' need to differentiate (and elevate) their product amid a glut of content—clearly has contributed to an increased public awareness of the showrunner figure and, with it, heightened coverage of them. (2015, 90)

The inclusion of this 'talent' on a project is seen as adding substantial commercial value and this is then leveraged as part of the sales pitch and branding for the show, though of course the failure of a show represents a huge reputational risk to the auteur. Because of this value and associated risk, these workers often command a high degree of creative autonomy and international mobility. Payment in exchange for their talent will represent a substantial percentage of the production budget but is also valuable leverage in attracting further investment.

While commissioners, controllers and 'the talent' might be the most visible forms of TV labour, the largest, most heterogenous group in the drama workforce is the production team, commonly referred to as 'the crew' or, in accounting terms, as the 'below the line' costs. These workers are routinely neglected in TV drama scholarship despite their centrality to the creative realisation of a project. While often grouped together in discussions of television labour, the nature of drama production means that multiple crafts contribute to the final product. A diverse group of skilled workers within costume, make-up, sound, camera, set and production design, lighting, location services, but also accountants, electricians, drivers and painters with relevant experience and qualifications, bring television drama to our screens. These workers add material and creative value to drama content, the sector and the places in which production takes place. Their skills, but also their availability, are a focal point for local policy-makers and industry in their lure to international productions.

However, the conditions under which this workforce operates is strikingly different from other sections of the television workforce. As Banks

(2010) points out, within academic study and creative policies: 'the craft worker is abstract labour, unnamed and uncelebrated'. As D'Arcy (2019) argues in respect of designers, the fruits of their labour is nonetheless integral to textual meaning and audience pleasure. Workers in the production stage are often an invisible part of the process regarded simply as 'labour in service of the artist, one who supports the "talent"' (Banks 2010, 312).[3] As their work is perceived as more routine, standardised and predictable, they are regarded as more amenable to reform and control within creative production. Consequently, this segment of the workforce is often subject to the flexible demands of major production companies and their projects, and, when necessary, made expendable.

Part of the precariousness inherent in television labour lies in the conditions under which television drama is made. Time and financial pressures mean that efficiency greatly affects the working culture (Blair 2001). Productions can be characterised by long working days on set or on location, which is one reason for mid-career attrition within the sector. For instance, in order to film a single episode of *Doctor Who* within a two-week deadline, the producers and directors will rely on the skills of a relatively well-established production team. For other dramas with equal demands around pace and costs, producers tend to hire people they know from a shallow talent pool, or those with widely recognised credentials who can demonstrate having worked previously on a successful drama. Here again, reputation becomes an important factor in the mobilisation of labour and in the ability of certain people to get access to these key occupational spaces. These conditions can also cultivate a culture of profound risk aversion when assembling a crew.

The pressure to achieve production efficiencies, coupled with informal recruitment and unpredictable labour demand, have led to diminishing employment security for production workers within the television sector. The contractual status of many workers further augments this precariousness. As in many other national contexts, the television industry in the UK is increasingly freelance with 39% of the television industry employed on a freelance basis (Creative Skillset 2015). This is significantly higher than the creative workforce average (24% in 2014) and is mainly

---

[3]Some of these workers will achieve the status reserved for artists due to their individual skill or competency in specific high-status crafts. Some will be well paid and enjoy a high degree of creative autonomy, while being recognised in various awards such as BAFTA's Television Craft Awards. However, these are in the minority.

concentrated to workers within the 'crew'. The rise in this contractual structure is due to a number of factors, including the project-based nature of the television work; the practices of indies who often rely on the flexibility granted by freelance labour; greater contractual flexibility in the wider services and knowledge-based economy; the lure of self-actualisation through being 'your own boss' and attempts to secure greater cost efficiencies within cultural production where craft labour is often regarded as a more flexible and controllable cost compared to marketing or talent costs. This can pose enormous challenges for workers trying to cultivate a stable income, but also for industry and policy-makers as they try to construct a responsive and flexible workforce with attendant challenges for training and skills development.

The impact of this structure is that the once-substantial power of unions within the sector has been curbed, enabling much greater wage flexibility in response to demand (Christopherson 2006). Nonetheless, unions representing the interests of production workers, such as BECTU in the UK and the IATSE in the US and Canada, do retain their voice, cultivating a collective professional structure and coordinating on behalf of members' interests. Equally, some workers have used online platforms to mobilise and draw attention to exploitative work practices, though Saundry et al. (2007) express concern about whether these isolated campaigning activities lead to substantive changes in working conditions.

Here, a wider tension reveals itself. On the one hand, there is the cooperation and stability needed to improve collective conditions and on the other, the need to cultivate one's own talent and reputation within a highly competitive market characterised by oversupply (Caldwell 2008). Television drama production operates within a reputational economy; the reputation of individual workers, organisations (including firms and broadcasters) and places are all integral to how value is attributed, realised and exchanged within this system. For workers, this entails specific forms of what we might term 'reputational capital'. Cronin (2016, 399) defines reputational capital as a distinct subtype of Bourdieu's wider symbolic capital which 'takes form through converging logics of distinctiveness and competition in neoliberalising society'. The cultivation and enhancement of one's reputation has become integral to the logic of career development for television workers, often to their own detriment. For example, the Canadian actor and #aftermetoo activist, Mia Kirshner, has noted how the working conditions of actors makes them more vulnerable to workplace sexual assaults: 'It's an industry where your reputation as being "likeable" – which means being agreeable and saying "yes" – matters. Doing nudity when you've agreed a no nudity clause. It often counts against you if you say no' (Huffington Post 2018). Moreover, within this reputational economy, the onus is on workers to secure and develop their careers through their networks and experience (Lee 2011; Hesmondhalgh and Baker 2008). Responsibility for progression and development, along with employment costs (for example, paying for insurance, sick leave or maternity leave) has shifted almost entirely to the individual worker.

It is this combination of precarious working, the need to cultivate reputational value and workplace individualisation that has created endemic inequalities in this labour market. A growing debate within the television industry and reinforced by academic research (Saha 2012; Friedman et al. 2016; O'Brien et al. 2016), relates to the material experiences of workers. Television's reputation as being a creatively fun and informal place to work masks the significant barriers to full participation for women, for black, Asian and minority ethnic (BAME) workers, for disabled workers, and for workers from disadvantaged socio-economic backgrounds.

For example, the prominence and success of women in television could be taken as evidence of the feminisation of the industry (Ball 2012) and the considerable gains made by female workers including writers such as Kay Mellor, Abi Morgan, and Heidi Thomas. Certainly the work of female producer-writers such as Sally Wainwright, Shonda Rhimes, Jane Campion, Camilla Hammerich, Lena Dunham and Susanne Bier is enjoyed by audiences worldwide. There has been an ascendency of female-centred prime-time dramas including *Prime Suspect* (1991–2006), *The Fall* (2013–2016), *Top of the Lake* (2013–present) *Scott and Bailey* (2011–present), *The Good Wife* (2009–2016) and *Orange Is the New Black* (2013–present). Additionally, women occupy an increasing number of senior roles. At the time of writing, Charlotte Moore is Director of Content at the BBC (2016–present), Alex Mahon is CEO of Channel 4 (2017–present) and Sharon White is Chief Executive of Ofcom (2015–present).

However, a number of scholars (Conor et al. 2015; Lotz 2010; McElroy 2017; O'Brien 2015; Hallam 2013) warn against attributing this development to a more inclusive working environment. Wing-Fai et al. (2015) argue that motherhood—but not fatherhood—is a key factor in understanding the persistence of gender inequalities in film and television. Women do 'get in' to film and television, but they still rarely 'get on' as well as their male peers; they are what Wing-Fai et al. (ibid.) call career 'scramblers'. This is often cited in terms of writers and directors who get fewer opportunities for funded development, a point starkly made in the Directors UK report *Who's Calling the Shot?*[4] It reported that the share of episodes directed by women within the form of drama and comedy between 2013 and 2016 increased from 14.1% of the overall amount, but to only 18.5%. These findings are echoed in research by the Writer's Guild, which found that only 14% of prime-time TV is written by women (Kreager 2018). Therefore, while some gains have been made, the full participation of women in television production, and drama specifically, is frustratingly slow. In her Steve Hewlett Memorial Lecture the BBC's Charlotte Moore surmised that here begins 'a very long journey to address a huge historical failing of female voices' in television (RTS 2018).

Prominent figures in television such as Christopher Eccleston, Lenny Henry, Julie Walters and Phil Redmond (the writer behind *Grange Hill* (1978–2008), *Brookside* (1982–2003) and *Hollyoaks* (1995–present)), have also highlighted publicly how increasingly rarefied roles such as scriptwriting and acting have become. For many working in creative professions, television drama has become an opportunity only afforded to the privileged few, namely white middle-class men:

> It used to be hard for everyone. Whereas now, it's still hard for everyone but it's a whole lot harder, quantifiably harder, if you happen to come from anything other than money and privilege. (Cadwalladr 2016)

This is supported by research from Friedman et al. (2016), which found that 73% of actor respondents were from backgrounds deemed to be 'middle-class', despite the fact this group makes up only around 29% of the whole population. The ubiquity of free labour within the television industry and wider creative sector make this even more problematic, with

---

[4] Such gendered exclusions are also notable in television scholarship. For example, of Manchester University Press's sixteen monographs in The Television Series, only one is on a woman writer (Hallam's 2011 *Lynda La Plante*). Only two of the eighteen The BFI TV Classics series is on female-centred dramas: Billson's 2005 *Buffy the Vampire Slayer* and Jermyn's 2010 *Prime Suspect*).

48% of creative workers having done unpaid work at some point in their career, up from 43% in 2010 (Creative Skillset 2015, 4).

To conclude, labour forms a vital, yet often overlooked, element in the production of drama content. There are distinct characteristics of television drama labour due to the risk and scale of drama's production and it is labour that is key to the realisation of drama's economic value and international mobility. It is workers, especially those who form the production crew, who routinely shoulder the risks of increased competition and casualisation within the television production landscape. Workers are persuaded to shoulder this risk and further self-commodify, partly due to the rhetoric put forward by governments and industry offering work that is self-actualising, flexible and even fun. Routine discrimination becomes difficult to counter within the informal, casualised network of television production.

SCREEN POLICY AND THE MARGINALISATION OF LABOUR

It is with these labour market tensions in mind that we now turn our attention to how both television work and the worker are framed, and subsequently mobilised, within policy structures. The television sector has been central to the development of the UK's creative economy, both because of its economic contribution, but also because of its successes within the export market.[5] A range of global drama successes, from *Poldark* (2015–present) to *Downton Abbey* (2010–2015), *Victoria* (2016–present) to *Doctor Who*, offer tangible evidence of the range, depth and commercial strength of the UK's television industries, and subsequently the creative and business talents of those working therein. Moreover, television drama presents a unique opportunity to sell Britain and its creativity to the world, and, increasingly, a domestic creative labour market is a vital asset to allow that ambition to be fulfilled. A critical mass of skilled indigenous workers is framed by national policy-makers as part of a transition to more complex economic outputs which will therefore spur greater value and growth. In the UK, public and private investment has been framed as the answer to many ills associated with the decline in manufacturing and to improve the capacity of

[5] In 2015–2016, international sales of UK-made shows rose 10% to a record £1.3bn, with sales to China rising 40% and by 16% to the US, the biggest market for British content (PACT 2017).

television production. For instance, investments in the Titanic Quarter (Belfast, Northern Ireland), Pacific Quay (Glasgow, Scotland), Salford Quays (Salford, Greater Manchester) and Roath Lock (Cardiff, Wales) were predicated partly on the claim that these capital projects would bring much-needed highly skilled jobs to these post-industrial areas. This extends beyond the UK, to the development of production centres in diverse areas such as South Africa, Toronto in Canada, the Gold Coast in Australia, testifying to the international mobility and homogeneity of such policy interventions (Druick 2016; O'Regan et al. 2010; Collins and Snowball 2015). Labour is increasingly framed within this policy context as part of the proposition to internationally mobile productions looking for skilled and cost-effective workers, as we will illustrate in the next chapter with the case of *Game of Thrones.*

While both UK and devolved policy-makers have embraced the creative industries, creative work and the experiences of individual workers are narrowly conceived and often marginalised. A rhetoric of meritocracy and entrepreneurship characterises policy discourse (Littler 2018). Where creative industries policy does engage with labour it is predominantly in positive, individualised and intrinsic terms (Banks and Hesmondhalgh 2009). Despite mounting empirical evidence, there is a marked reluctance among policy-makers to articulate and remedy the structural conditions of creative work such as the informal hiring practices and casualisation that lead to inequalities and precariousness. Within policy the main form of value to be delivered through the creative economy and television production is economic, either in the form of brand value to attract inward investment or the financial value of making and exporting content. McElroy (2016, 70) points to the weaknesses of this approach:

> When sustainability is equated with economic success, questions of diversity, cultural representation and the need to foster indigenous creativity risk being eschewed as outmoded concerns.

There is little concern within current policy frameworks for the quality of television jobs as part of a career over a lifetime. The development of a skilled television workforce is positioned solely in terms of an economic and industrial good (for example, the number of new or highly skilled jobs) rather than as a cultural resource or as a means to social reform.

There are several reasons for this limited conceptualisation of labour within policy. Unlike capital investment which can be measured, made visible and is immobile, the development of a creative labour force often requires intangible and long-term outcomes. Workers can easily leave and seek employment elsewhere meaning policy-makers have limited control. Further, the supply of labour requires long-term thinking and crosses many policy domains including education, business and culture. Creating joined-up policy in relation to creative labour presents a challenge to policy-makers as they attempt to harmonise various agendas.

One further reason for this policy 'blind spot' is the cyclical, project-based nature of TV production and unpredictability relating to the final product. For example, in 2015 the Welsh government proudly announced that it had helped to secure Wales as the site of production for *The Bastard Executioner* (2015), a drama from Kurt Sutter, show-runner of the highly successful series *Sons of Anarchy* (2008–2014). The majority of production crew for the series would be drawn from the local labour market, bringing both financial investment and the opportunity to work on a high-profile series. However, success quickly turned to disappointment when, due to subdued audience figures, the series was cancelled before the end of its first season. This highlights the volatility of the television drama market, the riskiness associated with investment and how factors outside the political sphere (in this case audience tastes) have a substantial bearing on long-term investment. Ultimately, building the capacity of the workforce and a sustainable sector relies on commissioning and audience tastes, and government policies have little control in determining this demand.

Within policy there is a well-established discourse of self-actualisation, creative autonomy and entrepreneurship that stifles critical discussion about the realities of work for most people in the industry, or the uneven experiences of work by different workers in that community. As with workers in the Hollywood film industry, the invisibility of television workers is often desirable and necessary for the continued exploitation of that labour, especially in the lure to foreign investment (Conor 2011). In order to appear attractive to international productions, labour costs must be kept low and workers acquiescent.

However, it is becoming increasingly difficult for policy-makers, regulators and broadcasters to ignore the structural inequalities in the labour market. Since 2017, Ofcom has published an annual diversity report on UK television broadcasting. Institutional policies have emerged to address skills and diversity thereby extending the range of investors in labour. Several sector-specific schemes, such as Creative Diversity Network's Project Diamond,[6] have emerged emphasising the reporting of labour data and transparency around who is in front and behind the camera. Yet despite these reports and initiatives, debates about inequalities and work conditions have had little impact on national policy. This presents a major risk to the goal of a sustainable, high-skilled production sector. Without a cohesive, medium-term strategy for enhancing skills and removing barriers to entry and retention within television production, these underlying structural weaknesses will remain.

DOCTOR WHO, BBC CYMRU WALES AND ROATH LOCK STUDIOS

> I think it really matters that production doesn't just all kind of land in one place, and particularly London. I think there is that feeling of wanting to show to the rest of the nation that there are really talented, creative individuals in different pockets all over the country. Symbolically it was really a sort of perfect timing that we opened this incredible new facility and I think it's really important in terms of the perception within Wales as well. It suddenly meant that drama in Wales was serious. (Interview with Head of Drama for BBC Cymru Wales 2013)

The BBC's drama studios in Roath Lock, Cardiff opened in 2012 at a cost of £20 million. These permanent, purpose-built studios house the production of some of television's most significant dramas, including *Doctor Who*, *Casualty* (1986–present) and the BBC's longest running television soap *Pobol y Cwm* (1974–present) made for S4C. The studios in Cardiff form part of the BBC's strategy for developing regional and national 'centres of excellence', and to leverage the talented workforce 'in pockets' throughout the country.

The studios are based in a large-scale creative development located in the former docklands of the Welsh capital. This development is a joint venture between the property developer, igloo, and the Welsh Government, and is intended as 'a hub for the creative industries, attracting like-minded individuals and companies to cluster around Roath

---

[6] Diamond is an online system used by the BBC, ITV, Channel 4, Channel 5 and Sky to obtain consistent diversity data on programmes they commission.

Lock, to encourage interaction and work more closely together' (Porth Teigr 2011). The co-locating of a studio, editorial offices and production services gives a focus for both financial and infrastructure investment in the local creative economy. As the above quote also suggests, it has important symbolic value within the TV sector, an internationally mobile value we've examined elsewhere (McElroy and Noonan 2016). In the context of this chapter, Roath Lock offers a strategic centre through which labour can be assembled, developed and managed. It offers an original case study of a strategic intervention in the creation of a sustainable labour market and the challenges therein.

An established, experienced but economically fragile, television sector existed in Wales prior to the opening of the Roath Lock studios. The longstanding existence of public service broadcasters (BBC Cymru Wales, ITV Wales and S4C) along with other bodies such as Ffilm Cymru Wales meant that there was an ecology of independent production companies. However, in the case of English-language drama production, Wales was largely operating as a service provider; as one of our interviewees explained it 'was more of a smash and grab type scenario, where drama companies would come in, film, and then go away again. Not leaving any real legacy except for quite significant spends in the areas that they set up production bases in' (Interview with Wales Screen Manager 2013).

The relaunch of *Doctor Who* by the BBC in 2005 was a profound turning point in the view of our interviewees, providing the catalyst in the transition to an expert and sustainable production workforce in Wales. The success of the series and its spin-offs (*Torchwood* (2006–2011) and *The Sarah Jane Adventures* (2007–2011), produced in-house by BBC Cymru Wales in Cardiff) along with the scale of production of the series, was crucial to securing the city's reputation for quality drama and therefore attracting further investment. Less than a decade later and confidence in the local labour market in Cardiff had grown:

> The first series I think of *Doctor Who* tended to bring in an awful lot of crews and facilities from London into Wales. I think in the middle of the first series, or at least the second series, a Welsh-based director was put on to direct the series of *Doctor Who* and then said "we need to be using Welsh-based people who I'm comfortable with and who I know can deliver exactly the same standards". You saw then Welsh-based crews coming on to *Doctor Who*. There's established companies being set up and they're

employing people from Wales. That definitely is significant impact with the BBC's Roath Lock. (ibid.)

This quote neatly illustrates a number of things. In the first instance, it highlights the role of commissioning on the fortunes of a labour market. Without the decision to relaunch *Doctor Who* and then produce it in Wales, subsequent developments within the local television industry might never have occurred and at the very least, progress would have been slower. The recommissioning of *Doctor Who* was a key moment for building a labour market within Wales and the development of material opportunities for Welsh television workers. Part of this is because of the success it would enjoy with domestic audiences. As discussed in Chapter 4, the appearance of a programme on UK network television garners visibility and enhances credibility for those associated with its production. Furthermore, *Doctor Who* sold widely in international markets, generating much-needed revenue; in 2010 it was BBC Worldwide's biggest-selling TV show internationally (Sweney 2011). It beamed images of Wales—albeit dressed as alien lands—to homes across the world, thereby setting the foundations for the kind of television tourism examined in Chapter 6. Wales had tangible evidence of its ability to produce commercially successful large-scale television.

The quote also highlights the porous nature of the television labour market. The previous chapter attended to the mobile nature of production and the practice of 'lift and shift'. However, labour is also mobile and may move to other sectors such as film and theatre, as well as to other places. There remains competition for investment and skilled television labour between Cardiff and nearby Bristol (see Genders 2019), cities close to each other and with vibrant creative sectors. Therefore, the contribution of *Doctor Who* to the local creative economy illustrates how one well-managed risk can transform the perceptions and fortunes of a labour market, but that momentum needs to be maintained if that reputation is to be solidified.

Our interviews reveal the strategic importance of high-*volume* productions not just high-*value* drama. A sustainable production centre, we argue, rests on the value of the returning series (or continuing series) to the labour market yet this is often overlooked by drama scholars. A returning series like *Doctor Who* is the staple of the television schedule and forms the foundations of a channel's offering. The returning series has substantial value in terms of labour development as it is routinised work, either weekly in the case of a soap opera or for certain months in the year (for instance season ten of *Doctor Who* was filmed from June 2016 to May 2017). This offers workers regular paid work, distinguishing it from the unpredictability of working on one-off productions. This value to workers and the region is reiterated by Northern Ireland Screen, the television and film agency of Northern Ireland, which partly financed *Game of Thrones*:

> Returning TV series allow for this kind of development which individual feature films or television productions do not; by sheer dint of it coming back on an annual basis, gradual professionalization and sustainability in the Northern Ireland sector are brought about. (Northern Ireland Screen 2016, 11)

While high-profile series like *Doctor Who* and *Game of Thrones* undoubtedly contribute to the scale and promotion of the local television industry, our empirical research also highlights the significant value of indigenous mid-range dramas and soaps (for example, *Casualty* and *Pobol y Cwm*) to labour markets. While they may have neither the same budget and prestige within the industry hierarchy nor secure significant international sales, they do a crucial job of skills development and building sustainability:

> Brian [Minchin] who's now the exec on *Doctor Who*, started as an assistant script editor on *Belonging*. You wouldn't necessarily have put him on *Doctor Who* straight off ... But if you can start him off on the next *Belonging* or *Baker Boys*, then people have that time to develop and understand and then become executive producer of *Doctor Who*. But you need that development and the sort of production for people to have that time to learn their craft and grow really. (Interview with BBC Cymru Wales Production Manager 2013)

Domestic returning series offer a space where workers can hone their talents, especially female and BAME creatives (McElroy 2016). This matters because of the cyclical and precarious nature of creative work and its expectation of on-the-job training. A space like Roath Lock brings together different productions, which can enable some forms of flexibility:

A lot of sound [recordists] have said, "I just can't do it anymore. I just don't want to work eleven-hour fortnights, sixteen-hour days and be away from my family". With women as well what we're having, "What do I do? Do I have a child or a career?" And one thing that we try to discuss with the BBC ... is to talk to them about job sharing, about flexible working. It can be complicated in some areas of drama, but I think they've been successful in *Pobol y Cwm* because it's a series where one person does one block and one the other ... there needs to be more imagination in terms of how can we be a more accessible workforce for people with childcare ... or other caring responsibilities because otherwise, we're losing the talent. (Interview with Manager of Welsh training and professional body CULT Cymru 2013)

High-volume productions allow staff to learn quickly, enabling them to 'find their feet' which 'gives you a more sustainable base from which to grow' (Interview with Chief Executive of Rondo Media 2013). As the development of skilled labour can be a lengthy process, shortages can be pronounced in the short term. Time is a crucial factor in labour development (that is, the time to learn a craft) but time is at a premium in the current landscape of drama production efficiencies.

There is distinct value within a mixed production economy offering different kinds of returning content, some of which is high-value and some high-volume—an argument we made in our evidence to the National Assembly for Wales inquiry on 'Film and major television production in Wales' conducted by the Culture, Welsh Language and Communications Committee (CWLC 2018). Less glamorous than international productions, returning domestic series are nevertheless frequently better able to deliver the objectives and promises of labour policy which is itself politically significant to post-industrial regions and nations. They remain consistently popular with audiences but also provide spaces where many workers develop their craft. Commissioning trends and tax incentives do not prioritise these and so they are often marginalised by television executives and overlooked in the creative industries agenda by policy-makers eager to claim the next television blockbuster like *Doctor Who* or *Game of Thrones*. Yet a sustainable production sector needs a well-developed tier of productions that offer workers a ladder of opportunity to move up and between types of production, thereby giving access to something closer to a structured career progression route within what remains a highly precarious labour market.

While we argue for different forms of intervention, we need to be cautious about labelling any of these as wholly transformative. Certainly, employment within the creative economy grew between 2011 and 2015 to account for 3.8% of all jobs in Wales, but Wales only accounts for 2.9% of UK creative economy jobs (DCMS 2016, 9). While the focus on drama in Wales may be creating new opportunities for workers who are cultivating a reputation in this area, there is still a relative scarcity of drama compared to factual or entertainment. Few local indies are drama experts. At the same time, not everything emerging from Roath Lock has been a success and the risk of commercial failure still remains a constant threat. The axing of the revived period drama *Upstairs Downstairs* (2010) by the BBC, which was filmed in purpose-built sets in the studios, highlights this pervasive risk within television production.

Nonetheless, our research demonstrates how interventions such as Roath Studios can produce material benefits for television workers and the wider industry. The studio space enabled occupational stability for some workers due to the range and proximity of productions housed there (McElroy and Noonan 2016). It enabled professional mobility for others, as some of the writers, actors and producers went on to work on other quality dramas. As detailed above, the career trajectory of one of the executive producers on *Doctor Who* was offered as evidence of the upward mobility and skills development enabled by returning dramas. This value is echoed in Eva Novrup Redvall's 2013 study of Danish television production within and for the public broadcaster, DR. Her interviewees credit the collaboration and confidence that emerged from DR's studios as an element in the success of 'Nordic noir' as a globally successful genre. Therefore, investment in studios can deliver value in terms of career stability and development, thereby building a critical mass of expertise which can be sold internationally.

For the wider industry, developments like the BBC's Roath Lock provides tangible evidence of a growing reputation for production which attracts further investment and enriches the pool of workers, from emerging young creatives to more prominent 'talent'. Two developments beyond Roath Lock demonstrate this value well. Firstly, in 2014 Pinewood, the UK's iconic film studios, opened its own studios in South Wales signalling its confidence in both the local workforce and the Welsh strategy for television industries, with the fourth series of *Sherlock* (2010– present). This was followed in 2015 by the 'return' to Wales of Julie Gardner and Jane Tranter, two senior executives credited partly with the relaunch of *Doctor Who*. Gardner and Tranter chose to locate their production company Bad Wolf in Wales and LA and leased their own studios, Wolf Studios Wales, reported to be the largest in Wales.[7] Reflecting on the move, Gardner said: 'Jane and I have filmed all over the globe and know, first hand, that the talent base in South Wales is world class. We are thrilled to be embarking on this new venture surrounded by such shared talent and passion' (Barraclough 2015). Capital investment projects like Roath Lock are an important resource in attracting and retaining forms of creative talent in a globally competitive market marked by a high degree of mobility. They are integral in this reputational economy to the branding of places like Wales as an excellent centre for drama production with opportunities for steady work and career progress.

Investments like Roath Lock also allow the concentration and monitoring of labour such as facilitating work experience, mapping career progression and identifying skills gaps. Indeed, at the time of the interviews many of our interviewees reflected on how the development of Roath Lock and its operating at full capacity also highlighted gaps in the labour market in Wales, especially around technical services (such as location managers and script supervisors) and other high-level skills (such as writers and producers with international credits). These roles, central to drama production, become vital in terms of a pipeline of work and in building the sustainability of the workforce including that located along the supply chain. As one interviewee commented, 'if you don't train your script editors, where do your next productions come from?' (Interview with BBC Cymru Wales Production Manager 2013). Roath Lock then becomes part of the rationale to extend and deepen training and development around specific valued functions. This also requires a 'growth coalition' (Christopherson 2006) of partners such as the broadcasters, independent production companies, education and skills providers (for example, Higher Education, Further Education, ScreenSkills), the trade unions, government and others. Reconciling these partners' different ambitions is challenging but necessary if long-term sustainability is to be achieved.

This is something reiterated by Jane Tranter in her 2019 Royal Television Society Cymru lecture. She linked the future of her independent

---

[7] The site for the Wolf Studios Wales has been acquired by the Welsh Government and will be initially leased to provide studio facilities for Bad Wolf's production slate as well as accommodating other major TV and film productions.

production company Bad Wolf to the development of the labour market in Wales:

> Bad Wolf can't deliver on its commitment to Wales - or reach its full potential - without drawing deeply on the talent, skills and creative energy of the community around us. Put simply, Bad Wolf won't flourish unless the industry around it does. [...]. Our belief was that the television industry here needed long-term investment in skills and the supply chain, and that should come from a partnership between the industry and government. Of which Bad Wolf is one small part in the chain. (Tranter 2019)

Tranter's argument is that independent production companies like Bad Wolf that are large-scale, internationally recognised homes to major global productions have a formal, anchoring role to play in the provision of a skilled, sustainable labour market through partnership with public bodies. As controversial beneficiaries of substantial Welsh government investment, Wolf Studios sits alongside Roath Lock as an example of how publicly funded studio space for drama provide a catalyst for production and the labour market. However, buildings in themselves will not deliver the kind of skilled, sustainable and inclusive workforces to which many in the sector seems genuinely to aspire. As indicated in our sustainability table (see Table 1.1) a thriving television production ecology requires cohesive interventions from a range of public bodies as well as support from commercial entities such as the independent production sector. In the next chapter, we turn our attention to other ways in which public bodies intervene in production, namely screen agencies and tourist boards.

REFERENCES

Ball, Vicky. 'The "Feminization" of British Television and the Re-traditionalization of Gender'. *Feminist Media Studies* 12, 2 (2012): 248–264.

Banks, Mark. 'Craft Labour and Creative Industries'. *International Journal of Cultural Policy* 16, 3 (2010): 305–322.

Banks, Mark and David Hesmondhalgh. 'Looking for Work in Creative Industries Policy'. *International Journal of Cultural Policy* 15, 4 (2009): 415–430.

Barraclough, Leo. 'Jane Tranter, Julie Gardner, BBC Execs Behind "Doctor Who," Launch Bad Wolf'. *Variety*, 27 July 2015. Accessed 25 May 2018.

http://variety.com/2015/tv/global/jane-tranter-julie-gardner-bbc-execs-be-hind-doctor-who-launch-bad-wolf-exclusive-1201549009/.

Blair, Helen. '"You're Only as Good as Your Last Job": The Labour Process and Labour Market in the British Film Industry'. *Work, Employment & Society* 15 (2001): 149–169.

Blandford, Steve. *Jimmy McGovern*. Manchester: Manchester University Press, 2013.

Boyle, Raymond. *The Talent Industry: Television, Cultural Intermediaries and New Digital Pathways*. London: Palgrave Macmillan, 2018.

Cadwalladr, Carole. 'Why Working-Class Actors Are a Disappearing Breed'. *The Observer*, 8 May 2016. Accessed 25 May 2018. https://www.theguardian.com/film/2016/may/08/working-class-actors-disappearing-britain-class-privilege-access-posh.

Caldwell, John Thornton. *Production Culture: Industrial Reflexivity and Critical Practice in Film and Television*. Durham: Duke University Press, 2008.

CAMEo. *Workforce Diversity in the UK Screen Sector: Evidence Review*. Leicester: CAMEo Research Institute, 2018.

Christopherson, Susan. 'Behind the Scenes: How Transnational Firms Are Constructing a New International Division of Labor in Media Work'. *Geoforum* 37 (2006): 739–751.

Collins, Alan and Jen Snowball 'Transformation, Job Creation and Subsidies to Creative Industries: The Case of South Africa's Film and Television Sector'. *International Journal of Cultural Policy* 21, 1 (2015): 41–59.

Conor, Bridget. 'Problems in "Wellywood": Rethinking the Politics of Transnational Cultural Labor'. *Flow Journal*, 19 May 2011. Accessed 25 May 2018. https://www.flowjournal.org/2011/05/flow-favorites-problems-in-wellywood-rethinking-the-politics-of-transnational-cultural-labor-bridget-conor-goldsmiths-college-university-of-london/.

Conor, Bridget, Rosalind Gill and Stephanie Taylor. 'Gender and Creative Labour'. *The Sociological Review* 63 (2015): 1–22.

Creative Skillset. 'The Creative Media Workforce Survey 2014'. 2015. Accessed 25 May 2018. https://www.screenskills.com/media/1559/creative_skillset_creative_media_workforce_survey_2014-1.pdf.

Creative Skillset. 'The Full Picture: The Demand for Skills in UK TV Production'. Creative Skillset, 2016. Accessed 25 May 2018. http://creativeskillset.org/assets/0001/8052/The_Full_Picture_-_The_Demand_for_Skills_in_UK_TV_Production.pdf.

Creative Skillset. 'High-End TV: Skills Research'. Creative Skillset, October 2017. Accessed 18 October 2018. https://www.screenskills.com/media/1564/hetv_skills_research_detailed_debriefkehg-1.pdf.

Cronin, Anne M. 'Reputational Capital in "the PR University": Public Relations and Market Rationalities'. *Journal of Cultural Economy* 9, 4 (2016): 396–409.

Culture, Welsh Language and Communications Committee (CWLC). 'Inquiry: Film and Major Television Production in Wales'. National Assembly for Wales, 2018. Accessed 6 November 2018. http://senedd.assembly.wales/mgConsultationDisplay.aspx?id=296&RPID=1013502703&cp=yes.

DCMS. 'Creative Industries Focus on Employment'. DCMS, June 2016. Accessed 18 October 2018. https://www.gov.uk/government/statistics/creative-industries-2016-focus-on.

Directors UK. 'Who's Calling the Shots?' August 2018. Accessed 31 October 2018. https://www.directors.uk.com/campaigns/gender-equality-in-uk-tv.

Druick, Zoe. 'Canadianization Revisited: Programme Formats and the New Cultural Economy of the Canadian Broadcasting Industry'. *Journal of Popular Television* 4, 1 (2016): 75–89.

Friedman, Sam, Dave O'Brien and Daniel Laurison. 'Like Skydiving Without a Parachute: How Class Origin Shapes Occupational Trajectories in British Acting'. *Sociology*, 28 February 2016. https://doi.org/10.1177/0038038516629917.

Genders, Amy. 'An Invisible Army: The Role of Freelance Labour in Bristol's Film and Television Industries'. University of the West of England, 2019. Accessed 15 May 2019. https://bristolfreelancelabour.files.wordpress.com/2019/05/uwe_genders_invisible_army_web_2019.pdf.

Hallam, Julia. 'Drama Queens: Making Television Drama for Women 1990–2009'. *Screen* 54, 2 (2013): 256–261.

Hesmondhalgh, David and Sarah Baker. 'Creative Work and Emotional Labour in the Television Industry'. *Theory, Culture and Society* 25 (2008): 97–118.

Huffington Post. 'Mia Kirshner and the Fight Against Workplace Sexual Harassment With #AfterMeToo'. Huff Post, 2018. Accessed 31 October 2018. https://www.huffingtonpost.ca/2018/09/09/mia-kirshner-aftermetoo-tiff_a_23520991/.

Jensen, Pia and Anne Marit Waade. 'Nordic Noir Challenging the "Language of Advantage": Setting, Light and Language as Production Values in Danish Television Series'. *Journal of Popular Television* 1, 2 (2013): 259–265.

Johnson, Beth. *Paul Abbott.* Manchester: Manchester University Press, 2013.

Kreager, Alexis. 'Gender Inequality and Screenwriters'. Writers Guild, 22 May 2018. Accessed 31 October 2018. https://writersguild.org.uk/wggb_campaigns/equality-writes/.

Lee, David. 'Networks, Cultural Capital and Creative Labour in the British Independent Television Industry'. *Media, Culture and Society* 33, 4 (2011): 549–565.

Littler, Jo. *Against Meritocracy: Culture, Power and Mobility.* London: Routledge, 2018.

Lotz, Amanda. *Redesigning Women: Television After the Network Era.* Urbana: University of Illinois Press, 2010.

Mann, Denise. "It's Not TV, It's Brand Management." In *Production Studies: Cultural Studies of Media Industries*, edited by Vicki Mayer, Miranda J. Banks and John Thornton Caldwell, 99–114. New York: Routledge, 2009.

McElroy, Ruth. 'Television Production in Small Nations'. *Journal of Popular Television* 4, 1 (2016): 69–73.

McElroy, Ruth. 'The Feminisation of Contemporary British Television Drama: Sally Wainwright and Red Production'. In *Television for Women: New Directions*, edited by Rachel Moseley, Helen Wheatley, and Helen Wood, 34–52. Abingdon: Routledge, 2017.

McElroy, Ruth and Caitriona Noonan. 'Television Drama Production in Small Nations: Mobilities in a Changing Ecology'. *Journal of Popular Television* 4, 1 (2016): 109–127.

Newcomb, Horace and Robert Alley. *The Producers' Medium*. New York: Oxford University Press, 1983.

Northern Ireland Screen. 'Adding Value: Volume 2'. 2016. Accessed 9 November 2018. http://www.northernirelandscreen.co.uk/wp-content/uploads/2017/01/new_3439864.pdf.

O'Brien, Anne. 'Producing Television and Reproducing Gender'. *Television and New Media* 16, 3 (2015): 259–274.

O'Brien, Dave, Daniel Laurison, Andrew Miles and Sam Friedman. 'Are the Creative Industries Meritocratic? An Analysis of the 2014 British Labour Force Survey'. *Cultural Trends* 25, 2 (2016): 116–131.

O'Regan, Tom, Ben Goldsmith, Ben and Susan Ward. *Local Hollywood Global Film Production and the Gold Coast*. St. Lucia, QLD, Australia: University of Queensland Press, 2010.

PACT. 'UK Television Exports 2015–2016'. 3 February 2017. Accessed 24 August 2018. http://www.pact.co.uk/news-detail.html?id=impressive-growth-in-uk-television-exports-up-10-to-1-326m.

Pateman, Matthew. *Joss Whedon*. Manchester: Manchester University Press, 2018.

Perren, Alisa and Thomas Schatz. 'Theorizing Television's Writer–Producer: Re-viewing The Producer's Medium'. *Television and New Media* 16, 1 (2015): 86–93.

Porth Teigr. 'BBC Roath Lock Studios Opened in Porth Teigr'. 2011. Accessed 9 November 2018. http://www.porthteigr.com/en/news-events/bbc-roath-lock-studios-opened-at-porth-teigr.

Preston, Alison. *Inside the Commissioners: The Culture and Practice of Commissioning at UK Broadcasters*. Glasgow: The Research Centre for Television and Interactivity, 2003.

Redvall, Eva Novrup. *Writing and Producing Television Drama in Denmark: From The Kingdom to The Killing*. Basingstoke: Palgrave Macmillan, 2013.

RTS. 'BBC's Charlotte Moore Highlights the Importance of British TV at the Steve Hewlett Memorial Lecture'. RTS, 12 October 2018. Accessed

26 October 2018. https://rts.org.uk/article/bbcs-charlotte-moore-high-lights-importance-british-tv-steve-hewlett-memorial-lecture.

Saha, Anamik. 'Beards, Scarves, Halal Meat, Terrorists, Forced Marriage: Television Industries and the Production of "Race"'. *Media, Culture & Society* 34, 4 (2012): 424–438.

Saundry, Richard, Mark Stuart and Valerie Antcliff. 'Broadcasting Discontent: Freelancers, Trade Unions and the Internet'. *New Technology, Work and Employment* 22, 2 (2007): 178–191.

Spicer, Andrew and Steve Presence. *Go West! Bristol's Film and Television Industries. Project Report*. Bristol: UWE, 2017.

Sweney, Mark. 'Doctor Who BBC Worldwide's Biggest-Selling TV Show Internationally'. *The Guardian*, 12 July 2011. Accessed 25 May 2018. https://www.theguardian.com/media/2011/jul/12/doctor-who-bbc-worldwide.

Tranter, Jane. 'RTS Cymru Annual Lecture 2019'. RTS, 5 March 2019. Accessed 14 March 2019. https://rts.org.uk/article/rts-cymru-annual-lecture-2019-jane-tranter.

Wing-Fai, Leung, Rosalind Gill and Keith Randle. 'Getting In, Getting On, Getting Out? Women as Career Scramblers in the UK Film and Television Industries'. *The Sociological Review* 63 (2015): 50–65.

Filmography

Bastard Executioner, The (FX Productions, Fox 21, Imagine Television 2015).

Brookside (Mersey Television 1982–2003).

Casualty (British Broadcasting Corporation 1986–present).

Doctor Who (BBC Wales 2005–present).

Downton Abbey (Carnival Films/ITV Studios 2010–2015).

Fall, The (Artists Studio/BBC Northern Ireland 2013–2016).

Game of Thrones (Home Box Office (HBO)/Television 360/Grok! Studio/Generator Entertainment/Bighead Littlehead 2011–2019).

Good Wife, The (Scott Free Productions/King Size Productions/Small Wishes/CBS Productions/CBS Television Studios 2009–2016).

Grange Hill (British Broadcasting Corporation/Mersey Television 1978–2008).

Hollyoaks (Lime Pictures/Mersey Television 1995–present).

Orange Is the New Black (Tilted Productions/Lionsgate Television 2013–present).

Pobol y Cwm (BBC Wales 1974–present).

Poldark (Mammoth Screen 2015–present).

Prime Suspect (Granada Television 1991–2006).

Sarah Jane Adventures, The (BBC Wales 2007–2011).

Scott and Bailey (Red Production Company/Ingenious Broadcasting/Veredus Productions/Ipomen Productions 2011–2016).

Sherlock (Hartswood Films 2010–present).

Sons of Anarchy (Sutterlnk/Linson Entertainment/Fox 21/FX Productions 2008–2014).

Top of the Lake (See-Saw Films, Escapade Pictures 2013–present).

Torchwood (BBC Wales/Canadian Broadcasting Company/BBC Worldwide Productions 2006–2011).

Upstairs Downstairs (BBC Wales Masterpiece 2010).

Victoria (Mammoth Screen/Masterpiece 2016–present).

CHAPTER 6

Cultural Intermediaries and the Value of *Game of Thrones*

Abstract This chapter uses cultural intermediation and the bodies that perform this work as an alternative and original point of entry into analysis of television drama production. We argue that cultural intermediaries such as screen agencies and tourist boards, while frequently neglected in TV drama scholarship, play a significant role in actualising economic, political and symbolic value. In order to do so, these intermediaries deploy a range of tools including public subsidies and digital branding strategies as they translate public policy into interventions intended to support and sustain the production sector. This chapter uses the case study of HBO's *Game of Thrones* to demonstrate how cultural intermediaries in Northern Ireland are attempting to restore the country's political and economic visibility in a global landscape.

Keywords Cultural intermediaries · Screen agencies · Tourism · Policy · *Game of Thrones* · Place branding · Public investment

Television drama production is part of an elongated chain of value involving a highly complex network of relationships. A range of institutions beyond the producer and broadcaster may intervene in the production of drama, and all seek to extract diverse forms of economic and cultural value. In this chapter, we will give greater attention to the broader range of stakeholders that bring television drama to our screens and make it meaningful. As a result of its scale and strategic value

© The Author(s) 2019   123
R. McElroy and C. Noonan, *Producing British Television Drama*,
https://doi.org/10.1057/978-1-137-57875-4_6

detailed in Chapters 2 and 3, TV drama production garners attention and thereby intervention from a range of stakeholders. From financial investment to production assistance, international branding to training initiatives, these interventions are provided by a network of public and private entities (including talent agencies, trade unions, local businesses, commercial investors and property developers, etc.). However, despite their ubiquity and significance within the value chain for television, these stakeholders are regarded as 'invisible hands' in the market for creative content (Roussel and Bielby 2015), invisible to audiences and often overlooked by television scholars.

This chapter, therefore, examines the activities and roles of two of these 'hands'—screen agencies and tourism boards—both of whom operate as cultural intermediaries invoking 'value' and 'sustainability' to justify their subsidies and interventions. We borrow Bourdieu's (1979) conceptualisation of 'cultural intermediaries' to analyse the differing forms of intermediation and the strategic benefits that screen agencies and tourism boards derive from their work. We use the example of Northern Ireland (NI), the base for the major television drama *Game of Thrones (GoT)*, to illustrate some of the industrial and cultural forms of value that are derived from television drama, partly illustrated in this quote from its Industry Minister in 2012:

> Throughout its lifespan it is likely that *Game of Thrones* will deliver the widest media exposure Northern Ireland has ever achieved outside of politics and the Troubles … Tourism Ireland and the Northern Ireland Tourist Board have, through this drama series, the opportunity to showcase many tourist attractions including the north coast, Castle Ward, the Mourne mountains, and Ballintoy to name but a few. In addition, Invest NI and Northern Ireland Screen are utilising *Game of Thrones* in their international sales pitch. … The credibility of association with international projects of this nature and scale has significant added value potential for the Northern Ireland economy. (Northern Ireland Industry Minister, Arlene Foster quoted by McAdam 2012)

We focus firstly on the work of the screen agency, Northern Ireland Screen, in attracting the programme makers to film in Northern Ireland and providing the requisite infrastructure for a production of this scale. Following that, we examine the tourist boards within Northern Ireland as they leverage value from the international success of the series and its imagery. In Chapter 4, we analysed public service values of place, understood as both serving local and regional needs and linking the local to the international. Here, we extend this to understand more thoroughly market-oriented values as places are imagined and remade through international branding and sales pitches to mobile productions and investors. We argue that these cultural intermediaries are a vital and overlooked link between sector strategy and the fictions that reach our screens.

Cultural Intermediaries Within the Television Industry

The role and power of cultural intermediaries was first theorised by Pierre Bourdieu in *Distinction: A Social Critique of the Judgement of Taste* (1979). Through a concern with the 'new petty bourgeoise' emerging in France in the years following the 1968 protests, Bourdieu brought attention to the range of social actors who operate in the provision of creative and cultural products. These actors mediate how goods are perceived by others, making symbolic production central to the work of cultural intermediaries (Bourdieu 1979; Maguire and Matthews 2014). We can see this work in activities like promoting a nation's creative outputs or testifying to the success of public investment. While the concept of cultural intermediaries has drawn criticism for its seeming imprecision, a framework which analyses cultural intermediation offers researchers a deeper understanding of the formation of value for particular products or practices and usefully prioritises issues of agency and power.

For us, cultural intermediaries are a structural and strategic part of mitigating some of the risk associated with making television drama, through ensuring the longer-term economic and cultural legacy to be leveraged from employment and fan tourism. Fully leveraging value from drama requires a 'growth coalition' (Christopherson 2006) comprising various stakeholders with a vested interest in leveraging the returns provided by television drama to their locale. One of the key tasks is to articulate a carefully curated image of a nation and its national identity, as international visibility and distinction are important operating logics within neoliberal markets. For this reason, cultural intermediaries often work beyond the jurisdiction of cultural policy alone, transcending domains of economy, culture, and labour. The outcome of this negotiation is that cultural intermediaries have become increasingly embedded within economic development and urban policy agendas, especially in the context of the post-industrial city (see Christophers 2008; O'Connor 2015). Television drama is an important strategic vehicle for garnering such visibility and securing diverse forms of value.

This wider context of economic growth, creative innovation and urban development occupied by cultural intermediaries can be identified in the policy landscape of Northern Ireland (NI). Peace remains a fundamental precondition of NI's ability to nurture an economically viable creative sector. Three decades of violent conflict in the region, often referred to as 'the Troubles',[1] meant that by the end of the century, the NI economy was devastated by a high unemployment rate, educational disadvantage and social exclusion (Buchanan 2014). Peace in the region nurtured the framing of a 'New Northern Ireland' which had tangible value in terms of enabling *some* economic recovery along with tentative attempts to bridge cultural and social divides (ibid.). A number of cross-border partnerships and agencies were formed, dedicated to leveraging the economic and cultural opportunities afforded by peace. A process of urban regeneration centring on drama production, Titanic Studios, accompanied that agenda (Ramsey 2013).

However, for cultural intermediaries working within NI, history and social identity continue to feature prominently in the post-conflict era and sectarian divisions continue to thwart the policy process.[2] One of the outcomes of this unique political context and the ongoing conflicts over the symbolic culture of NI, is that there is a relatively weak national cultural policy framework (Ramsey and Waterhouse-Bradley 2018), the mechanism by which many screen-based policy initiatives emerge.

---

[1] The Troubles refers to the conflict which took place in Northern Ireland from 1968 to 1998. Over 3600 people were killed and thousands more injured in a country with a population of approximately 1.5 million. Violence was commonplace on the streets of Northern Ireland, with some violence taking place in Great Britain and the Republic of Ireland. Several attempts to find a political solution failed until the Good Friday Agreement, which restored self-government to Northern Ireland and brought an end to the Troubles, though the economic, socio-political and culture legacy of that conflict endures today.

[2] At the time of writing, Northern Ireland's devolved executive had collapsed, partly as a result of disagreement over legislation for the Irish language, while Brexit also threatens the screen sector. In the 2016 referendum, Northern Ireland voted 56% to remain and 44% to leave the European Union, undermining the Democratic Unionists, the main party in NI, which backed Brexit. The post-Brexit customs system remains a particularly contentious issue within the UK's negotiations with the EU.

Therefore, the decision by HBO, the US makers of *Game of Thrones*, to base their production in NI and to do much of the principal photography for the show around the region took many by surprise. Here emerges the vital role of the screen agency, Northern Ireland Screen, and their intercession in bringing the makers to Northern Ireland.

Leveraging Value Through Screen Agencies

Screen agencies have become prominent pillars of publicly funded intervention in the film and television industry.[3] Indeed, the agency model has become a legitimated and transferable policy structure, as most nations now have some form of screen support network, often nationally and/or regionally centred. A selective list demonstrates the geographical spread and scale of these bodies: Screen Ireland, Film France, screen.brussels (Belgium), Croatian Audiovisual Centre, New Zealand Screen Association, Screen Australia, Utah Film Commission (US), Massachusetts Film Office (US), the Colombian Film Commission, Guadeloupe Film Commission and Kenya Film Commission. These actors contribute to decisions about what gets made and seen, and they offer a diverse range of services including, databases of filming locations, advice on working with heritage organisations, landowners and police services, location scouting, support in recruiting freelance crew, provision of hospitality and accommodation and providing information about and access to film and television studios. In addition, many of these agencies also offer, directly or via fellow agencies, production and development funding.[4] They address the challenge of converting disparate production *activity* into a sustainable production *industry* (Christopherson and Rightor 2010) with the aim of converting

[3] In 2018 the authors were awarded funding by the Arts and Humanities Research Council (AHRC) for a two-year research project on 'Screen Agencies as Cultural Intermediaries: Negotiating and Shaping Cultural Policy for the Film and TV Industries within Selected Small Nations' (AH/R005591/1). More information about that research can be found at www.smallnationsscreen.org.

[4] In Wales, for example, these functions exist in separate bodies. Wales Screen operates as part of the Welsh Government's Creative Industries Sector team to encourage incoming film and television production to use locations, crew and facilities in Wales. Meanwhile, Ffilm Cymru Wales supports Welsh or Wales-based writers, directors and producers with development and production funding, industry assistance and mentoring opportunities. In 2019, McElroy became Chair of Ffilm Cymru.

short-term contractual exchange to long-term sustainability that allows
critical mass in both economic opportunity and cultural representation.
Their overall purpose is to improve the effectiveness of public funding for screen-based industries. In doing this, intermediation becomes
a highly political act (see O'Connor 2015) framing what is regarded as
having economic value and what is considered culturally significant.

One of the most obvious extensions of the remit of screen agencies concerns the nature of the *screen*. While film has historically been
their key area of intervention, high-end television drama has become a
central object of investment as a result of its scale, value and visibility.
These intermediaries further legitimise investment in high-end television drama, differentiating it from other forms of television content (for
example, soaps and game shows) as this subgenre is seen to offer unique
opportunities to build indigenous screen industries. The possibility to
exploit forms of Intellectual Property (IP) is an attractive incentive to
screen agencies and they are key brokers within multiplatform and digital expansion, bridging traditional and emerging forms of content. The
extension of television brands into gaming and apps, means that these
forms has received more strategic attention and intervention from screen
agencies. Value is extracted by these agencies through a range of screen-
based devices, as we see later in our example of the *Game of Thrones* app.

In the UK a complex, regional infrastructure has been developed with
both the UK and national Scottish, Welsh and Northern Irish devolved
governments, investing in television drama production as part of their
broader creative industries policies. Screen agencies such as Creative
England, Creative Scotland, Northern Ireland Screen, Screen Yorkshire,
and Wales Screen compete with one another to provide film and television productions with support and resources to attract investment into
their own nation or region. These agencies also invest strategically to
support and develop indigenous productions. However, in the UK in the
last two decades, screen agencies have been subject to the shifting tides
of political support as the policy landscape has been substantially rear-
ranged in pursuit of competitive advantage, creative innovation and value
for money (see Schlesinger et al. 2015, 3; Hesmondhalgh et al. 2015).

Direct funding of creative projects is often the most visible form
of support from screen agencies, either in the form of co-financing or
a recoupable loan. In the UK, screen agencies distribute funding from

two primary sources, government and the National Lottery.[5] Northern Ireland Screen offers production funding to 'assist in completing budgets on productions which are almost fully financed' and which 'contribute to building a sustainable screen industry in Northern Ireland' that can demonstrate a 'direct economic benefit to the region' (Northern Ireland Screen 2018). This funding role has become more pronounced as complex forms of co-production and co-financing become increasingly normalised within the drama production process, as discussed in Chapter 3. The agency attempts to evaluate the riskiness of the project, relying on its internal expertise about what will find an audience domestically and sell internationally. In this way the agency becomes an investor in the television industry on behalf of the government and its taxpayers, potentially exercising invisible forms of power through its decision-making and support.

A further role of screen agencies is to promote the quality of the country's creative capacity outside its borders, thereby attracting inward investment to the locale. Indeed, screen agencies play a leading role in attracting lucrative forms of large-scale inward investment associated with filming Hollywood movies or big-budget television dramas. Value is derived from this promotion in multiple ways, as this executive at the Øresund Film Commission in Denmark understands:

> We create value first of all because filmmakers come here and work, that makes sense. Secondly, we create value because we are branding our country. So, if a big international show is shooting here it is seen by maybe 40 million people who are watching Netflix shows on average. ... So that of course creates awareness of our country and brands our country very well, that we get our shows out on Netflix and HBO. (Interview with Øresund Film Commission 2012)

This role, and the value derived, is neatly illustrated in the production history of *Game of Thrones*.

In 2007 the American premium cable and satellite television HBO optioned George R. R. Martin's fantasy novel *A Song of Ice and Fire*

---

[5] Set up in 1994, the National Lottery donates £33 million from lottery ticket sales each week to a wide range of good causes. There are currently 12 Lottery funders who decide which projects have successfully applied for a grant, including the British Film Institute, Creative Scotland and the Arts Council of Northern Ireland.

and began to seek a location for filming the pilot episode. Scotland, Morocco and Ireland were all touted as filming locations and many countries and their screen agencies attempted to woo the programme makers. However, in 2009, HBO confirmed that principal filming would begin the following year at the Paint Hall studio facilities in the Titanic Quarter of Belfast—a regenerated development built around the former Harland and Wolff dockyards. The Paint Hall, which operates as a base for principle filming on *GoT*, offers tangible evidence of the economic prospects of the creative industries (see Ramsey 2013).[6] Like Roath Lock Studios in Wales in the previous chapter, the developer, Harcourt Developments, sees this facility and the content that emerges as emblematic of a new creative economy in Northern Ireland, 'one of the world's largest urban waterfront regenerations schemes' (Titanic Quarter 2018). It purposefully incorporates the legacy of the city's maritime and industrial past through the iconic structures of Samson and Goliath, the remaining Harland and Wolff cranes. Here, economic and urban development become wrapped up in cultural policy and creative production, extending the network of stakeholders involved in leveraging value from television drama.

Attracting *GoT* was a coup for NI as it was the first time that a TV production of such substantial scale had been filmed in the region. Northern Ireland has a long history of domestic television production, but it is also a relatively small television market in terms of access to advertising revenue, licence fee revenue and pools of talent—all of which matter as smaller nations compete in a global marketplace (see Ferrell Lowe and Nissen 2011; Hjort 2011; Iosifidis 2007). At the same time, local commissioning from broadcasters like the BBC was falling (Ramsey and Waterhouse-Bradley 2018). A returning television series of the scale proposed for *GoT* would potentially reverse the fortunes of the region and would be an essential component in any plans for sustainability. Therefore, the pitch to HBO was driven by economic ambition and necessity.

While it may be an apocryphal story, the decision to locate *GoT* in the region is partly credited to a visit at the time by the First Minister

---

[6] In 2012 the Paint Hall was expanded and rebranded as Titanic Studios, illustrating the transition from old to new modes of production. The building is currently on licence to Northern Ireland Screen.

(Peter Robinson) and Deputy First Minister (Martin McGuinness) to Los Angeles to meet with the programme makers (Belfast Telegraph 2009). However, more significant was the promise of substantial public investment through Northern Ireland Screen (Ramsey et al. 2019).[7] Through the strategies *Driving Global Growth* (Northern Ireland Screen 2010) and *Opening Doors* (Northern Ireland Screen 2014), Northern Ireland Screen positions itself as delivering on the twin aims of an economic return on public investment and developing the skills base of the television and film industries as a route to long-term sustainability of the creative economy. The agency, with the approval of the NI Executive, played a crucial role in providing financial subsidies to the *GoT* project and enticing the makers to the country (Ramsey and Waterhouse-Bradley 2018; Ramsey et al. 2019). Northern Ireland Screen invested £13.75m of public money in the first six seasons as part of the package of incentives to the programme makers (Girvin 2016). HBO was also able to access the benefits of the UK's High-end Television Tax Relief, discussed in Chapter 2.[8] For HBO, the global corporation behind *GoT*, such public funds were an important lure to the region, and, controversially, would continue long after the financial risk to the company of this production had passed (Ramsey et al. 2019). This exemplifies how contemporary television drama, specifically high-end drama, has been increasingly reoriented as a vehicle for economic policy by national and regional players such as screen agencies as they seek to secure international investment in their locale.

Northern Ireland Screen considers the investment to have been worthwhile, having returned £146m to the local economy in terms of services and tourism (Girvin 2016). While Northern Ireland is the

---

[7] Established in 1997 as the Northern Ireland Film Commission (NIFC), Northern Ireland Screen evolved from the Northern Ireland Film & Television Commission (NIFTC) to reflect its growing remit for all screen-related industry including digital content and gaming. Core funding for the agency is provided through Invest NI, itself a publicly-funded body designed to attract foreign investment and build local industry.

[8] In this scheme companies filming in the UK can claim a maximum of 25% relief on qualifying expenditure. To qualify for tax reliefs, a scripted television project must have a minimum core expenditure of £1 million per broadcast hour. Productions must also pass a cultural test or qualify through an internationally agreed co-production treaty certifying that the production is a British programme. The production company can claim a payable cash rebate of up to 25% on UK qualifying expenditure.

show's production base, it is not the only beneficiary as filming has also been carried out in Malta, Croatia, Iceland, Morocco and Spain, often filming simultaneously in more than one country. The Croatian Audiovisual Centre (the screen agency of Croatia) reported that in 2014 *GoT* spent around €5.7 million during filming in their country, including employing 300 local film professionals and extras (HAVC 2014). Therefore, while public investment is high, countries and their screen agencies are keen publicly to promote the return on investment and the financial reward resulting from their interventions.

Such claims of a return on investment are common rationalising tools in this production landscape. However, Christopherson and Rightor (2010, 349) warn that due to difficulties in capturing data effectively 'assertions of the efficacy of subsidy programs as an economic development tool remain speculation'. It can be difficult to assess accurately the volume of jobs and value created by filmed projects as these are often transitory and short-term. Nonetheless, this kind of macro data is captured and promoted and becomes an important justification of public spending. Even where evidence exists, the conclusions are not always positive. Ramsey et al's. (2019) analysis of NI's screen highlights that while the agency's 'approach might be a standard economic measurement appropriate to the assessment of public spending, it might ultimately be a limited one in terms of measuring societal benefit', especially in terms of long-term employment. Evidence from Canada also suggests that interregional competition has increased the profits of transnational media firms, rather than building a sustainable regional industry (Christopherson 2006). The contractual relationship (now ended) between Welsh Government and Pinewood Studios has also been the subject of a critical report from National Assembly Wales' Public Accounts Committee, which raised questions about the transparency of the relationship and its delivery against a promised £90 million anticipated value to the Welsh economy. Therefore, despite the significant sums of public monies being directed to private media companies under the frame of sustainability and economic return, the data suggesting that places receive an effective return on their investment is contentious. This has significant implications for the scrutiny of cultural intermediaries that facilitate this investment and for the modes of assessing the effectiveness of their interventions.

PUTTING PLACES 'ON THE MAP': TOURISM AND TV DRAMA

In Northern Ireland a growth coalition of Northern Ireland Screen, Invest NI and Tourism Northern Ireland (the main tourist board for the region), have been central to leveraging value from television and film production. These agencies collaborate on initiatives, co-fund projects and liaise with third-party providers. This illustrates the complex interconnection between production services and tourist bodies as tourism strategy and its imagery have become enmeshed with other forms of diplomacy and promotion around trade, investment, competition and export. These efforts are often associated with enhancing the international credibility and political influence of the local in the face of globalising forces (Anholt 2010; Urry 2011). In some locales there is increased dependence on tourism as an alternative source of income, particularly following a decline in the local manufacturing industry. Like television production, the tourism sector is seen as lucrative and attractive to policy-makers keen to secure the financial returns of the international tourist as part of broader international relations policy. Television, in particular drama, offers tourism bodies a tangible resource to help put their place 'on the map' (McElroy 2011).

In a highly mediatised global tourism market, the imagery and visual resources of television drama are both highly valued and increasingly mobile (Urry 2011). Film and television have global power to render locales distinctive. Britain, like many other places, has long been a location for filming television and has more recently leveraged the benefits of television-related tourism across a range of places and landmarks often beyond metropolitan areas, for example: Dorset (*Broadchurch* (2013–2017)), Cardiff (*Doctor Who* (2005-present), *Torchwood* (2006-2011)), Lerwick (*Shetland* (2013–present)), Cornwall (*Poldark* (2015–present), *Doc Martin* (2004–present)), Liverpool (*Peaky Blinders* (2013–present)) and Oxfordshire (*Midsomer Murders* (1997–present), *Lewis* (2006–2015), *Inspector Morse* (1987–2000)). Aside from an initial location fee, policy-makers and local stakeholders are alert to the exposure that television can bring in the longer term, especially if the series in question is renewed across multiple seasons. TV-related tourism multiplies the effect of the initial investment through supporting hotels, restaurants, transport and retail, along with their workers. For instance, the combined value of the Swedish and British versions of *Wallander* (2008–2016) is estimated at £17.5 m in promotional value for Ystad in Sweden, the onscreen location of both series (Euroscreen 2014). For those places that can secure a successful production, television drama offers financial reward and a unique set of symbolic resources which can continue to pay, even once the production crews have left.

However, while tourism may be a desirable legacy of television drama production it can be problematic, and temporary, if achieved at all. Some content resonates more 'touristically' than others and there can be associated problems relating to misrepresentation, inauthenticity and congestion (see Blandford et al. 2010; O'Regan et al. 2010; Toft Hansen and Waade 2017; Waade 2016). Some stories, representations and tourism may be undesirable, such as the emergence of 'narcotours' in Columbia following the success of the Netflix series *Narcos* (2015–2017) (*The Guardian* 2018). Success can also bring 'over-tourism'—for example, in Dubrovnik in 2015, there were some 300 tours related to *Game of Thrones*; in 2017 there were 4500 tours, causing local officials to put in place some restrictions (Santora 2018). Moreover, programme makers often have little loyalty to a place and may move if it doesn't suit their needs. A further challenge is that, creative industries and tourism policy domains frequently sit in separate departments of government, making a cohesive policy approach less likely. Therefore, few destinations retain control over how and to whom their place is presented on screen and so tourism agencies are an important broker in securing some forms of control, albeit often in limited ways.

Game of Thrones has been placed at the centre of tourism policy-making in Northern Ireland by the various bodies working in the region and this seems to be delivering some returns.[9] Overall visitor numbers in the year to September 2017 increased by 11% with an increase of 18% in overall visitor spend. This makes tourism worth £679m to the NI economy as external visitors have reached record levels (Department for the Economy 2018). There are a number of reasons for the centrality of *GoT* to tourism in Northern Ireland. It enjoys a significant production

[9] Northern Ireland has a complicated tourism infrastructure emanating directly from its history and unique policy landscape characterised by cross-border cooperation and trans-jurisdictional organisations. Tourism is the responsibility of the Department for Enterprise, Trade and Investment (DETI) at Northern Ireland Executive level. The department is the sponsor of Tourism Northern Ireland whose work is focused on promoting domestic tourism and visitors from the Republic of Ireland. Following the 1998 Good Friday Agreement another body, Tourism Ireland, was formed and DETI co-sponsor this agency (along with the Department of Transport, Tourism and Sport in the Republic of Ireland) which is responsible for promoting Northern Ireland in Great Britain and in overseas markets.

budget, setting it apart from many productions, especially indigenous drama.[10] This financial input means that alongside studio filming in vast and complex sets, location filming is also possible in the countryside, secluded bays and numerous castles of Northern Ireland, all of which are central to the show's narrative setting. As discussed in Chapter 4, the potential for sweeping location shots and significant set pieces adds to the 'quality' drama label and offers exceptional imagery foregrounded in many promotional campaigns.

TV-related tourism offers a particular mode of exchange and so, as well as places realising the benefits, there is specific value for the makers of *GoT*. Tourism can augment brand value and revenue streams for television networks like HBO during a time in which new challengers enter the sector (Thomas 2012). While *GoT* may enjoy exceptional budgets, this comes at a cost to the length of its seasons, which are relatively short (10 episodes in seasons 1–6). Therefore, viewers of the series must be kept engaged from one season to the next—fan conventions and their pilgrimages to locations help to cultivate and maintain interest between seasons. While some attempts to build engagement are discernible in HBO's history, much of its previous content does not lend itself to 'typical character licensing' (VP of Global Licensing HBO cited in License Global 2013)—a growth area for many drama producers. Therefore, licensing, to include event-based extensions such as a *Game of Thrones* touring exhibition, is important to keep fans engaged in what is not an abundantly lengthy series.

There are also logistical reasons for leveraging *GoT* as a tourism resource. The programme is immensely popular with US audiences[11] and American visitors are critical to Irish tourism as a substantial diaspora travel to Ireland in the hope of reconnecting with their genealogy.[12]

---

[10] In its earlier seasons, *Game of Thrones* episode cost on average approximately £4.5 million to make. However, the sixth season had a budget of £75 million for 10 episodes. The most expensive episode of that season involved one of the largest battle scenes ever filmed for television, which involved 600 crew members, 500 extras, 70 horses, 25 stunt performers, four camera crews and 25 days of shooting (Hibberd 2016).

[11] In the US, linear ratings of the Season 7 finale of the series recorded 12.1 million viewers, making it the most-watched episode in the history of the series. This represents a 36% increase over the Season 6 finale, which drew 8.9 million viewers in 2016 (Otterson 2017).

[12] The US is the second largest market for tourism on the island of Ireland. Between 2012 and 2016 there was a 60% increase in American holidaymakers, which led to a 70% rise in revenue. Tourism Ireland's strategy aims to build further, with a target to grow American visitor numbers by 23% by 2021. The strategy has been developed in close

The close proximity of filming locations to each other has undoubted convenience for the production team, but also lends itself to a comprehensive tourist itinerary. Visitors, especially those travelling from overseas, have the opportunity to see a number of their favourite places during a single visit. Tangentially, this disperses the benefits beyond Belfast to rural locales, supporting a variety of rural enterprises, giving a rationale for public support and a route to decentralising the economic value of TV drama production.

HBO permitted Tourism NI to use trademarks, logos and images from the show, and these have been a central element in campaigns orchestrated by the tourist board. One of the most prominent was the 'Doors of Thrones' campaign—a series of *GoT*-themed hand-carved wooden doors placed around Northern Ireland. In 2015 Storm Gertrude knocked down several trees at the Dark Hedges, one of the most iconic filming locations of *GoT* and a firm fan favourite. Discover Northern Ireland used the fallen trees to create a series of doors featuring imagery from the series, then placed the 10 doors around Northern Ireland in bars or restaurants near the main shooting location of *GoT*, further enhancing visitor itineraries and embedding *GoT* in the cultural fabric of the country.

The use of *GoT* imagery within these campaigns is significant to the touristic story of NI. While violence is part of the public image of NI, television drama can shift violence from fact to fiction. Tzanelli (2016) argues that places with complex socio-political histories, such as NI, attempt to replace historical trauma with fantastic scenarios which are more palatable to tourists. Histories of civil war are replaced by other imagery which is then converted into tourist commodity. The official history and image of NI is sanitised though there is considerable difficulty in controlling the experiences of tourists, especially in a digital age.

Digital technology, especially social media, is a growing element within attempts to enhance the visibility and mobility of both places and television drama. In the context of *GoT* social media is important because of demographics of the audience (i.e., digitally literate young people) but also because the programme has a strong presence

co-operation with Tourism NI and Fáilte Ireland, as well a wide range of industry partners in NI and the US (McKeown 2018).

on the internet (for example, an official website and numerous fan blogs). However, social media can also work against a place and undermine some of its attempts to position itself in an international market. Two incidents illustrate this. In an interview circulated online Kit Harington, one of the lead actors on *GoT*, described the tourist board (Tourism NI) as celebrating three things: the Europa Hotel as 'the most bombed' in Europe, the Titanic which sunk on its maiden voyage, and *Game of Thrones*, 'the most depressing show' on television (BBC 2015). Furthermore, in 2014 a number of stories appeared in the press and were shared online suggesting that the showrunners were not happy staying in Belfast during filming. In an interview with Vulture magazine, HBO's president of programming admitted D. B. Weiss and David Benioff, found living in Belfast 'a personal challenge; I don't think they contemplated when we initially found our location in Belfast, what that meant for them personally ... Belfast is not the most cosmopolitan of cities to spend half of the year. ... I don't think they have a hard time, but the good news is work keeps them busy, let's just say that' (Marotta 2014). A grovelling apology followed: '*Game of Thrones* could not have become the show it is today without the incredible partnership between HBO and Belfast. From the government's co-operation to the hundreds of workers on set to the scenic beauty, Northern Ireland lives in every episode of the series' (Ferguson 2014).

Despite these risks, social media has become an essential way for television drama to enhance interactivity, participation and value. For instance, the 'movie map' has long been an integral element of film-inspired tourism—its evolution into an app propels it into the digital age. Apps are increasingly part of the offering to visitors as a way of leveraging control and augmenting the tourist experience. For example, Highclere Castle, the site of *Downton Abbey* (2010–2015), offers smartphone users an app which includes photographs of the castle, video interviews and historical information. The *GoT* app also provides illustrated maps, production imagery and details of filming locations in Northern Ireland, 'designed to give you information on which scenes were filmed where, as well as help the visitor to Northern Ireland navigate those filming locations which are accessible to the public' (Northern Ireland Screen Commission Ltd 2018).[13] While they are often an

---

[13] The *Game of Thrones* app was developed in Northern Ireland (by NI studio The Design Zoo) with credited funding from Northern Ireland Screen and Invest NI, again demonstrating the collective intermediary stakeholders in drama.

important part of the tourist proposition, preservation of filming sets is not always possible (for example, where shooting took place in public areas or where CGI has been used as a more cost-effective resource). Apps, therefore, are able to use digital imagery to fill the gap. The *GoT* app provides directions to the location and a 360-degree virtual tour of the location, allowing even non-visitors to step into the location. Through these activities digital maps provide 'new layers of cultural meaning and alternative modes of affective engagement' (Leotta 2016).

This layering of meaning raises its own problems becoming another tool in the redefinition and construction of a place's identity. For instance, little of the recent history of NI appears on the *GoT* app, suggesting such digital resources are 'geared towards the mastery, packaging and international promotion of Northern Ireland landscapes as the only part of "Irish character", habitus and history worthy of salvation from oblivion' (Tzanellii 2016, 62). The complex reality of NI is swept away, a critique which can be much applied to much nation branding. Certain contexts, histories and meanings are formulated by (often invisible) technology companies that finance and distribute these apps (see Leotta 2016; Tzanelli 2016). This commodification risks oversimplifying the socio-political nature of territorial space. In the context of *GoT*, this means the power to define NI partly resides with transnational media corporations like HBO.

SELLING NORTHERN IRELAND TO THE GLOBAL MARKET

This chapter uses cultural intermediation and the bodies that perform that work as an original and alternative point of entry into analysis of television drama production. It argues for greater attention to the ways cultural policies are realised in practice and specifically to the role that cultural intermediaries play within the provision and international mobility of television drama. We draw critical attention to the differing and complex roles of screen agencies and tourist bodies. While the work of these bodies may take place at different stages in the television value chain, these organisations enact a range of brokerage functions and negotiate complex organisational partnerships within and around drama production. Their activities demonstrate the tangible merging of economic and cultural value in the current creative industries framework and within television production specifically.

Despite the international mobility of certain cultural policy interventions, our attention to Northern Ireland reminds us of the salience of national specificities. For example, peace was a vital precursor to the offer made by Northern Ireland Screen to the US makers of *Game of Thrones*. While some of the appeal was aesthetic, there were also important commercial rationales, including local financial incentives, the promise of improved facilities, a skilled but affordable labour market, and amenable local authorities. These elements are central to the lure to internationally mobile productions and the provision of contemporary television production within many national contexts. Undoubtedly, there is some benefit to NI with the appearance of the locale on screen, even if it is presented within the *GoT* narrative as the Seven Kingdoms. Awareness within the industry of NI as filming location has grown and data highlights an upturn in tourism. However, there is a significant cost to the public in terms of financial investment and disruption (for example, road closures or overcrowding at key locations). Further, the announcement that the series was to conclude after its eighth season demonstrates the temporality of television production as a resource and raises questions about the long-term legacy of this investment.

There is a dearth of analysis about the long-term impact of television investment on the cultural or economic sustainability of a nation or locale. Equally, there is little sustained scrutiny of the funding arrangements which redirect tax-payer money to global players like HBO (itself a subsidiary of Time Warner). The long-term trend towards deregulation within the television sector means that, under the terms of commercial sensitivity, neither these conglomerates nor their subsidiaries are required to supply data about such investments. This also raises problems about how public bodies and governments actually calculate the value of their intervention (see Ramsey et al. 2019; Turnbull and McCutcheon 2017) and therefore the effectiveness of intermediaries like screen agencies. The perception of television as prestigious and lucrative legitimises such commercial and political decisions, yet the risks of such investment remain obscure. Some of this concern was made visible by the Welsh Assembly committee on Culture, Welsh Language and Communication when in 2018 it launched an inquiry asking, 'whether the Welsh Government's multi-million-pound investments are delivering value for money'. Embedded within the inquiry were concerns around the transparency and cultural impact of the government's investment decisions (CWLC 2018). The Welsh Government's investment in attracting the well-known British film and television studio, Pinewood, to Wales and the operation of its Media Investment Budget both attracted much criticism from stakeholders.[14] Therefore, we conclude by arguing that greater accountability and attention to power is needed, especially in the redistribution of public money into the hands of privately owned media conglomerates. Whether this happens depends on the appetite of policy-makers and regulators to challenge their own well-established norms for assessing and attributing value to television drama content and its production.

REFERENCES

Anholt, Simon. *Places: Identity, Image and Reputation*. Basingstoke: Palgrave Macmillan, 2010.

BBC. 'Kit Harington Apologises for Joke About Belfast Tourism'. 30 April 2015. Accessed 18 November 2018. https://www.bbc.co.uk/news/uk-northern-ireland-32536468.

Belfast Telegraph. 'US Television Pilot, Game of Thrones, to be Filmed in Belfast'. *Belfast Telegraph*, 21 April 2009. Accessed 25 May 2018. http://www.belfasttelegraph.co.uk/entertainment/film-tv/news/us-television-pilot-game-of-thrones-to-be-filmed-in-belfast-28521759.html.

Blandford, Steve, Stephen Lacey, Ruth McElroy and Rebecca Williams. 'Screening the Nation: Wales and Landmark Television'. Report for the BBC Trust/Audience Council Wales, 2010. http://culture.research.southwales.ac.uk/screeningthenation/.

Bourdieu, Pierre. *La distinction: critique sociale du jugement* [Distinction: A Social Critique of the Judgement of Taste]. Paris: Editions de Minuit, 1979.

Buchanan, Sandra. *Transforming Conflict Through Social and Economic Development: Practice and Policy Lessons from Northern Ireland and the Border Counties*. Manchester: Manchester University Press, 2014.

Christophers, Brett. 'The BBC, the Creative Class, and Neoliberalism in the North of England'. *Environment and Planning A* 40 (2008): 2313–2329.

Christopherson, Susan. 'Behind the Scenes: How Transnational Firms Are Constructing a New International Division of Labor in Media Work'. *Geoforum* 37 (2006): 739–751.

Christopherson, Susan and Ned Rightor. 'The Creative Economy as "Big Business": Evaluating State Strategies to Lure Filmmakers'. *Journal of Planning Education and Research* 29 (2010): 336–352.

---

[14]At the time of writing the committee had yet to publish its final report from that inquiry.

Culture, Welsh Language and Communications Committee (CWLC). 'Inquiry: Film and Major Television Production in Wales'. National Assembly for Wales, 2018. Accessed 6 November 2018. http://senedd.assembly.wales/mgConsultationDisplay.aspx?id=296&RPID=1013502703&cp=yes.

Department for the Economy. 'Tourism'. Accessed 13 October 2018. https://www.economy-ni.gov.uk/topics/tourism.

Euroscreen. 'The Real Value of Having a Hit Film or Tv Show in Your Town'. 13 November 2014. Accessed 18 November 2018. http://euroscreen.org.uk/?p=2425.

Ferguson, Amanda. 'Game of Thrones Staff Happy in Belfast: HBO Boss Sorry for Panning City'. *Belfast Telegraph*, 17 June 2014. Accessed 18 November 2018. https://www.belfasttelegraph.co.uk/news/northern-ireland/game-of-thrones-staff-happy-in-belfast-hbo-boss-sorry-for-panning-city-30359224.html.

Ferrell Lowe, Geogory and Christian Nissen. *Small Among Giants: Television Broadcasting in Small Countries*. Göteborg: Nordicom, 2011.

Girvin, Sara. 'Game of Thrones Brings Estimated £150 m to Northern Ireland'. BBC, 11 July 2016. Accessed 18 November 2018. https://www.bbc.co.uk/news/uk-northern-ireland-36749938.

HAVC. 'Croatian Film Industry Profit Doubles This Year'. *Hrvatski Audiovizualni Centar* (HAVC), 26 September 2014. Accessed 25 May 2018. http://www.havc.hr/eng/info-centre/news/media-on-game-of-thrones-set-croatian-film-industry-profit-doubles-this-year.

Hesmondhalgh, David, Kate Oakley, David Lee and Melissa Nisbett. *Culture, Economy and Politics: The Case of New Labour*. Hampshire: Palgrave Macmillan, 2015.

Hibberd, James. 'Game of Thrones: Battle of the Bastards by the Numbers'. *Entertainment Weekly*, 16 June 2016. Accessed 25 May 2018. http://ew.com/article/2016/06/16/game-thrones-battle-bastards-numbers/.

Hjort, Mette. 'Small Cinemas: How They Thrive and Why They Matter'. *Mediascapes*, Winter 2011. Accessed 8 November 2018. http://www.tft.ucla.edu/mediascape/Winter2011_SmallCinemas.html.

Iosifidis, Petros. 'Public Television in Small Countries: Challenges and Strategies'. *International Journal of Media and Cultural Politics* 3, 1 (2007): 65–87.

Leotta, Alfio. 'Navigating Movie (M)apps: Film Locations, Tourism and Digital Mapping Tools'. *M/C Journal* 19, 3, 2016. Accessed 25 May 2018. http://journal.media-culture.org.au/index.php/mcjournal/article/view/1084.

License Global. 'The Reign of HBO's Game of Thrones'. 13 June 2013. Accessed 13 November 2018. https://www.licenseglobal.com/magazine-article/reign-hbos-game-thrones.

Maguire, Jennifer Smith and Julian Matthews. 'Are We All Cultural Intermediaries Now? An Introduction to Cultural Intermediaries in Context'. *European Journal of Cultural Studies* 15, 5 (2012): 551–562.

Maguire, Jennifer Smith and Julian Matthews (eds). *The Cultural Intermediaries Reader.* London: Sage, 2014.

Marotta, Jenna. HBO's Michael Lombardo on More Game of Thrones, the Future of MaddAddam, and Why American Gods Is a No-Go. *Vulture,* 11 June 2014. Accessed 18 November 2018. https://www.vulture.com/2014/06/hbo-american-gods-what-happened.html.

McAdam, Noel. 'Game of Thrones pumped £43 m into Northern Ireland's Economy, and More Could be on the Way'. *Belfast Telegraph,* 16 May 2012. Accessed 20 June 2017. http://www.belfasttelegraph.co.uk/entertainment/film-tv/news/game-of-thrones-pumped-43m-into-northern-irelands-economy-and-more-could-be-on-the-way-28749710.html.

McElroy, Ruth. '"Putting the Landmark Back into Television": Producing Place and Cultural Value in Cardiff'. *Place-Branding and Public Diplomacy* 7, 3 (2011): 175–184.

McKeown, Gareth. 'Visitors to Northern Ireland Are Now Spending £2.7 m a Day'. *Irish News,* 2 February 2018. Accessed 12 July 2018. http://www.irishnews.com/business/2018/02/02/news/ambitious-plans-to-boost-american-tourist-numbers-by-a-quarter-by-2021-1247067/.

National Assembly for Wales, Public Accounts Committee. 'The Welsh Government's relationship with Pinewood'. February 2019. Accessed 28 March 2019. http://www.assembly.wales/laid%20documents/cr-ld12165/cr-ld12165-e.pdf.

Northern Ireland Screen. 'Driving Global Growth: Celebrating Our Culture, Enhancing Our Children's Education, Boosting Our Economy'. 2010. Accessed 15 November 2018. https://www.nibusinessinfo.co.uk/sites/default/files/NI_Screen_strategy_DRIVING_GLOBAL_GROWTH_2010-14.pdf.

Northern Ireland Screen. 'Opening Doors: A strategy to Transform the Screen Industries in Northern Ireland'. 2014. Accessed 12 November 2018. http://www.northernirelandscreen.co.uk/wp-content/uploads/2017/01/Northern-Ireland-Screen-Annual-Report-and-Financial-Statements-2013-14.pdf.

Northern Ireland Screen. 'Funding'. 2018. Accessed 15 November 2018. http://www.northernirelandscreen.co.uk/funding/production-funding/.

Northern Ireland Screen Commissioning Ltd. 'Game of Thrones Locations'. Computer Software, *Apple App Store.* Vers 1.3, 2018.

O'Connor, Justin. 'Intermediaries and Imaginaries in the Cultural and Creative Industries'. *Regional Studies* 49, 3 (2015): 374–387.

O'Regan, Tom, Ben Goldsmith, Ben and Susan Ward. *Local Hollywood Global Film Production and the Gold Coast.* St Lucia, Australia: University of Queensland Press, 2010.

Otterson, Joe. 'Game of Thrones' Season 7 Finale Draws Record 16.5 Million Viewers'. *Variety,* 28 August 2017. Accessed 18 November 2018.

https://variety.com/2017/tv/ratings/game-of-thrones-season-7-finale-ratings-2-1202540601/.

Ramsey, Phil. '"A Pleasingly Blank Canvas": Urban Regeneration in Northern Ireland and the Case of Titanic Quarter'. *Space and Polity* 17, 2 (2013): 164–179.

Ramsey, Phil and Waterhouse-Bradley, Bethany. 'Cultural Policy in Northern Ireland: Making Cultural Policy for a Divided Society'. In *The Routledge Handbook of Global Cultural Policy*, edited by Victoria Durrer, Toby Miller and Dave O'Brien, 195–211. Abingdon: Routledge, 2018.

Ramsey, Phil, Stephen Baker and Robert Porter. 'Screen Production on the "Biggest Set in the World": Northern Ireland Screen and the Case of *Game of Thrones*'. *Media, Culture and Society* (2019): 1–18. https://journals.sagepub.com/doi/10.1177/0163443719831597.

Roussel, Violaine and Denise Bielby (eds). *Brokerage and Production in the American and French Entertainment Industries*. London: Lexington Books, 2015.

Santora, Marc. 'Throngs Enticed by "Game of Thrones" Threaten a Magical City'. *The New York Times*, 19 August 2018. Accessed 12 October 2018. https://www.nytimes.com/2018/08/19/world/europe/dubrovnik-croatia-game-of-thrones.html.

Schlesinger, Philip, Melanie Selfe and Ealasaid Munro. 'Curators of Cultural Enterprise: A Critical Analysis of a Creative Business Intermediary'. Hampshire: Palgrave Pivot, 2015.

Titanic Quarter. 'About'. 2018. Accessed 18 November 2018. http://titanic-quarter.com.

The Guardian. 'Narcotours: Netflix Fans Uncover the Real Life of Pablo Escobar'. *The Guardian*, Video, 4 October 2018. Accessed 16 November 2018. https://www.theguardian.com/world/video/2018/oct/04/narcotours-narcos-netflix-fans-uncover-the-real-life-of-pablo-escobar-video?CMP=share_btn_link.

Thomas, Lynnell. '"People Want to See What Happened": Treme, Televisual Tourism, and the Racial Remapping of Post-Katrina New Orleans'. *Television and New Media* 13, 3 (2012): 213–224.

Toft Hansen, Kim and Anne Marit Waade. *Locating Nordic Noir: From Beck to The Bridge*. Cham, Switzerland: Palgrave Macmillan, 2017.

Turnbull, Sue and Marion McCutcheon. 'Investigating Miss Fisher: the Value of a Television Crime Drama. *Media International Australia* 164, 1 (2017): 56–70.

Tzanelli Rodanthi. 'Game of Thrones to Game of Sites/Sights Framing Events Through Cinematic Transformations in Northern Ireland'. In *Event Mobilities: Politics, Place and Performance*, edited by Kevin Hannam, Mary Mostafanezhad and Jillian Rickly, 52–67. Oxon: Routledge, 2016.

Urry, John and Jonas Larsen. *The Tourist Gaze 3.0*. London: Sage, 2011.
Waade, Anne Marit. 'Nordic Noir Tourism and Television Landscapes: In the Footsteps of Kurt Wallander and Saga Norén'. *Scandinavica* 55, 1 (2016): 41–65.

Filmography

Broadchurch (Kudos Film and Television, Imaginary Friends, ITV—Independent Television 2013–2017).
Doc Martin (Buffalo Pictures/Homerun Productions 2004–present).
Doctor Who (BBC Wales 2005–present).
Downton Abbey (Carnival Films/ITV Studios 2010–2015).
Game of Thrones (Home Box Office (HBO)/ Television 360/ Grok! Studio/ Generator Entertainment/Bighead Littlehead 2011–2019).
Inspector Morse (Zenith Entertainment/Central Independent Productions/ Carlton UK Productions/WGBH 1987–2000).
Lewis (Granada Media/Granada Television/ITV Productions/ITV Studios/ WGBH 2006–2015).
Midsomer Murders (Bentley Productions/ITV—Independent Productions 1997–present).
Narcos (Dynamo/Gaumont International Television/Netflix 2015–2017).
Peaky Blinders (Tiger Aspect Productions 2013–present).
Poldark (Mammoth Screen 2015–present).
Shetland (BBC Scotland 2013–present).
Torchwood (BBC Wales/Canadian Broadcasting Company/BBC Worldwide Productions 2006–2011).
Wallander (Zodiak Entertainment/ARD Degeto Film/BBC Scotland/Film I Skane/Left Bank Pictures/TV4/WGBH/Yellow Bird 2008–2016).

CHAPTER 7

Power and Sustainability in TV Drama Production

Abstract This book focuses on the specific experiences and structure of local production and considers its relationship to global markets and domestic players such as PSBs. This leads us to conclude the book with a call for urgent and profound attention to power and sustainability. Power within the TV industry remains consolidated to a few key players and issues relating to the prominence and discoverability of content testify to the ongoing struggles and imbalances that characterise the television production landscape. We also critique the ubiquitous concept of sustainability as one which emphasises economic growth as the only view of progress or innovation. We propose the necessary conditions for creating a truly sustainable local production ecology and we argue for reinvigorating notions of television drama as a public good.

Keywords Sustainability · Prominence · Discoverability · Innovation · Diversity · Public service broadcasting

Drama is a form beloved by television viewers. Most people can enthuse about their favourite drama as a 'national treasure' and are keen to recommend a series as 'must see' to their family and friends. Drama is at the cornerstone of viewers' affection for television as a medium and it is embedded in the daily discussions of millions of viewers. At the time of writing (early 2019), those conversations ranged from the casting of Jodie Whittaker as the thirteenth incarnation of the Doctor in *Doctor*

© The Author(s) 2019

R. McElroy and C. Noonan, *Producing British Television Drama*,
https://doi.org/10.1057/978-1-137-57875-4_7

Who (2005–present) and the eager anticipation of the final season of *Game of Thrones* (2011–2019), to the public conversations on transgender identity following the transmission of the ITV drama *Butterfly* (2018). Television drama is at the centre of our daily lives and cultural conversations.

Drama is also one of the most prized forms in the television industry, offering considerable strategic value to diverse stakeholders within and outside the television market, including national governments. Ratings, brand enhancement, artistic success, awards and being part of the public discourse can all be leveraged from a successful drama. However, this value is in spite of the considerable riskiness of its production. Drama is one of the most expensive, most time-consuming and most labour-intensive television forms to produce. It requires the skills of many different workers and significant amounts of capital which may or may not deliver a return on investment. Consequently, the stakes are high for those who commission, make and distribute drama.

Within the TV industry itself there is considerable nervousness that the present era of abundance is also paradoxically an era of dramatically declining television consumption by young people. What television is and what it will become is at the heart of this debate. The history of television reveals that this is an industry that has always evolved responding to new technological affordances, cultural shifts and wider, often disruptive, political environments. What television—and therefore television drama—will become is not something anyone can predict with certainty. As researchers we are disinclined to future-gazing. However, it is clear that the industry itself, as well as policy-makers and regulators, need to be ambitious in positively reconceiving television beyond the existing infrastructure of the broadcast era. Undoubtedly, there are reasons for optimism not least in the evident enduring appetite people have for consuming well-told stories. This fundamental human desire is not disappearing. However, the challenge is to be genuinely creative in building a diverse and sustainable industry that can harness the value of new distribution routes to offer a more, not less, inclusive set of voices. Moreover, it means retaining the ambition and legacy of British television's radical storytelling exemplified in the rational of Channel Four's very establishment. Practically this means commissioners need to trust writers whose stories do not neatly conform to dominant neoliberal narratives of individualism (see Forrest and Johnson 2017; Malik and Nwonka 2017). Television scholars play a vital role in holding the industry to account publicly. As educators, our role also entails a commitment to making television production a more inclusive space for our students, many of whom aspire to be television professionals in the future.

INNOVATION IN TELEVISION DRAMA

Innovation has long been a feature of drama as a way to enhance distinctiveness in a competitive television landscape and as a way to cement the relationship with audiences. Creative forms of storytelling and emergent technologies deepen viewers' engagement with the content and create new opportunities for stories to be experienced and shared. For example, there is growing creative and economic value being derived from online drama and web series. Both formats are maturing and are coming to the fore in terms of innovative storytelling and industrial practice. A growing professionalisation of online drama over the past decade has unsettled preconceived ideas of 'professional' and 'amateur' within television production with content often distributed freely through ad-supported platforms like YouTube, giving all storytellers potential access to global audiences.

For those working in non-anglophone contexts, distributing drama online offers the opportunity to stake out their place in a crowded market. In a global and technological context dominated by English, this kind of content enhances the vitality of a language and makes visible other cultural markers. Part of this new trend can be seen in the phenomenal success of Korean dramas, often distributed internationally through online streaming services and made accessible to new audiences via subtitles which are crowdsourced from fans (Maybin 2018). In this way, online drama is a potentially rich creative domain for the mobility and normalisation of diverse languages and cultural identities.

Online dramas have developed their own aesthetic styles, often appearing as short-form content targeted to a digitally savvy audience of young people. Success in this area has also seen many of these titles cross over into television. For example, the US web series *Broad City* (2014–2019) was initially developed and independently produced for YouTube from 2009 to 2011 before being picked up by Comedy Central. For this reason, online dramas are increasingly being supported through the same mechanisms as traditional television drama. Alongside drama for transmission on traditional channels and in regular formats, Screen Australia funded *Life of Jess*, an ongoing web series comprising five 7–10-minute episodes and premiering in August 2018 on YouTube to an audience of over 400,000 subscribers (Screen Australia 2018) with some concluding that growth in this sector is 'shaking up Australia's screen industry' (Swinburne and Fabb 2017).

However, this innovation is not restricted to freelancers and independent companies many of whom are still challenged by the need to accrue new skills in their workforce and the need to secure business models and revenue streams that could support this new form of production. Public service broadcasters are also mobilising these online series as a route to engaging young audiences and as an innovative response to declining budgets. Like *Broad City*, *Fleabag* (2016–present) is a female-written and female-led comedy drama series initially produced for the digital channel BBC Three in a co-production agreement with Amazon Studios. Following its success on iPlayer it then moved to the mainstream channel BBC Two. *Fleabag* also exemplifies the way online drama is being used as a site for content and talent development by traditional broadcasters. Phoebe Waller-Bridge the creator of *Fleabag*, went on to write and produce the hugely successful drama *Killing Eve* (2018–present) for BBC America based on novels by Luke Jennings.

Elsewhere, one of the biggest successes in online European drama has been the Norwegian series *SKAM* (2015–2017). Produced by the public service broadcaster NRK, the storyline was revealed in real time via video clips, chat messages and pictures, inviting the audience to comment and engage. The series broke all streaming records in Norway and has grown to be an international phenomenon, the format having sold to France, Germany, Italy, the US and with subtitled clips of the series having been viewed 180 million times on Weibo in China (Max 2018). Outlining the value of SKAM to NRK, Andersen and Sundet (2019) point to two ambitions for this series: to reconnect with young audiences (especially those in the 10–13 age range) who NRK and other broadcasters struggle to routinely engage and to provide innovative content not likely to be available elsewhere. Digitisation and new competition have led PSBs like NRK and the BBC to produce short-form drama tailored to online streaming, capitalising on a digitally savvy audience adept at 'second screening' (Wilson 2016), with potentially unlimited ancillary content in the form of fan comments and interactions. While this form is still evolving, it illustrates some of the changes occurring in the production model for television drama which also entails reimagining what drama as a form is and can be. Formal innovations have the potential to deepen further the cultural value of drama on screen.

Interactive media forms like *SKAM* and the Netflix drama *Black Mirror: Bandersnatch* (2018) (a film which asks the audience to make a choice at various points which affects the storyline) also demonstrate the potential for forms of screen innovation more akin to gaming. The games industry has mastered the storytelling and technological infra-structure needed to help audiences navigate their path through nar-ratives. These interactive stories provide viewers with the chance to be part of the drama and offer greater control of the story deepening their engagement with the content and the platforms. Television producers still have much to learn from other screen sectors on how to use emerg-ing technologies like virtual, augmented and mixed reality in a genuinely meaningful way. Indeed, increasing emphasis is being placed on research and development across the screen sector as public bodies such as the UK Arts and Humanities Research Council and Innovate UK invest sub-stantial public funds into collaborative innovation projects within existing creative clusters and with a view to audiences of the future.[1]

However, behind greater personalisation lies myriad forms of active data collection and surveillance. This collection of 'big data' turns pas-sive viewing into active experiences, and the potential for disrupting and intervening in viewer habits is not fully visible or yet appreciated. This further accentuates arguments about what may be lost when high degrees of personalisation create a filter of content contributing to 'big datasets' and through which taste and demand can be projected (boyd and Crawford 2012; Michalis 2018). Therefore, we argue that drama scholarship needs a greater awareness of the politics and power of digital distribution especially given its semblance of data-driven certitude that is both quantifiable and impartial, and that is actively shaping the provision of drama content.

---

[1] The AHRC Creative Clusters programme has invested £80 million in eight creative research and development partnerships across the UK geared at bringing together crea-tive industries with arts and humanities researchers. The Audience of the Future (AoF) demonstrator programme is an £18 million investment in industry-led consortia to cre-ate new immersive experiences to be tested with large audiences. McElroy is Co-Director of Clwstwr (one of the Creative Cluster partnerships based in Cardiff City region) and a Co-Investigator with the Moving Image AoF Demonstrator.

Why We Still Need PSB in a Netflix Era

As teachers of television drama, we know that there is a seismic shift afoot in the consumption of television drama. Ask a class of nineteen-year-olds what they most enjoy watching and the chances are that most of them will refer to Netflix in their answer. The penetration of Netflix into the UK is deep, especially among younger subscribers. Netflix's ambition for growth with older viewers is in turn driving its commissioning and acquisition strategy. But once everyone who is inclined to subscribe for £5.99 per month has done so, where then for Netflix especially as the market for streaming platforms becomes saturated? By way of contrast, many of our students claim to watch very little linear television and they appear, superficially, to have little loyalty for the BBC, though Channel 4's youth drama like *Misfits* (2009–2013) and *Skins* (2007–2013) tend to elicit more lasting appreciation. Dig a little deeper, however, and what emerges is that landmark dramas such as *Sherlock* (2010–2017) come high on the list of what they are watching on Netflix. Yet rarely do they regard those dramas as the product of public service broadcasting, still less does it inspire any compulsion to purchase a license fee. At this point of disruption, it is easy to imagine that Netflix and other SVoDs will take over the world while PSBs, looking ever more outdated, will wither on the vine. This is one possible scenario, but it is not the most likely nor, more importantly, is it what will best serve the public interest.

The concept of public service, we argue, remains every bit as valid today as it did at the point of the BBC's establishment. Without broadcasters committed to the public interest, we risk eroding our democracy turning opinion into nothing more than a unit of economic value. Serving the public entails at the very least an aspiration to include all members of the public in imaginative debates about the society we live in, the relationships we want to have, and the conflicts we want to resolve. As Malik argues, how 'public service television responds to various social identities, including race and ethnicity, tells us how they are culturally organized, produced, and communicated to the nation and beyond' (2013, 227). Television drama is uniquely well-placed as a form to give voice to competing world views and experiences in ways that educate and inform us by entertaining us first and foremost. Drama's focus on character, a long-standing feature of British television fiction, enables us to enter the hearts and minds of people we do not know; to make us see the world through eyes that are not our own. Such plurality of vision and voice is integral to the ethos of public service broadcasting.

At the heart of PSB's ethos lies the public—the array of audiences who pay for and enjoy the dramas they watch, discuss and watch again and again. Repeat viewings evidence the deep affection and meaning audiences attach to drama. The vast archives of PSBs are a public, cultural resource, not just a major asset from which to leverage revenue. We know from our research that audiences remain attached to local stories that speak to their lives and concerns. Television drama's intimacy and proximity to its audience is something PSBs have often been able to exploit effectively. Digital technologies that bring content into our lives in ever more personal ways needs to be harnessed to this wider cultural purpose. Audiences are among the most powerful ambassadors for content; ignoring or excluding segments of the public from the offering of television drama is not only socially detrimental it also risks the very future of broadcasters themselves.

At the same time, PSB's contribution to the television industry lies in its relationship with workers. Local commissioning, content quotas, public accountability, along with structured training and development opportunities are just some of the ways that PSBs contribute to the development of the television industry. There is no obvious alternative, single source of these interventions and so they fulfil a key place in the local production ecology. As our empirical research demonstrated in Chapter 5, television production is characterised by different relationships to power, partly emanating from the precarious conditions of employment. The sector, led by the PSBs, has responded with efforts such as Project Diamond (Creative Diversity Network 2018). However, for these to be successful there will need to be more normalised and diverse representations on screen and fewer obstacles to meaningful participation off-screen. Although there are still plenty of criticism to be made of the PSBs, many of which we outlined in Chapter 4, we judge as vital the role that PSBs have in creating and maintaining the labour force as a route to preserving the quality of drama made in and from the UK.

In contrast, commercial online services such as Netflix, Amazon Prime and Apple are global firms that are inherently driven by profit-based business models where driving subscription to dominate markets is the main concern. For Amazon and Apple, television content is simply an add-on to their core technology business and so both have access to large amounts of capital and a well-established user base. Furthermore, unlike public service and commercial broadcasters in the UK, these global platforms operate in the television market while remaining relatively free from regulation by Ofcom. They are beneficiaries of substantial public investment in digital infrastructure in the form of broadband and, soon, 5G, and in their content provision through their use of the high-end tax relief scheme for instance. SVoD services have not had to invest directly in new affordances for the benefit of the public in the way that the BBC, for example, did in leading 'digital switchover'. As we argue throughout this book, wider public, cultural and socio-economic imperatives are not their concern.

Therefore, if we want to be able to enjoy a wide array of different types of drama geared to a diversity of audiences and providing long-term professional careers and businesses to regions and nations with sustainable production industries, then we need an invigorated and innovative public service media to emerge from this moment of disruption.

However, there are significant challenges to PSBs. As outlined in Chapters 2 and 3, the emergence of new digital pathways to content, the technological capacity to provide on-demand services, and arrival of new players have radically altered the ecosystem in which television drama is produced and distributed. New industry structures do not necessarily lead either to radical change, as Johnson (2019) demonstrates, or to a more democratic or diverse media. Entrenched forms of power continue to impinge on whose stories matter, how they get made and who gets to see them. As television scholar Amanda Lotz reminds us:

> Although expanded viewer sovereignty still seems possible in this nascent stage of post-network era, the history of distribution tells a different story. All too frequently, emergent technologies provide multiplicity and diversity in their infancy, only to be subsumed by dominant and controlling commercial interests as they became more established. (2014, 165)

A major challenge for policy-makers, regulators and PSBs themselves is to harness the potential of new technologies in ways that extend and enhance their core public purpose. Therefore, what is clear is that while *some* power has indeed transferred to new players in this age of uncertainty, public broadcasters still have a vital role to play. Within industry and policy discourse the concepts of 'choice' and 'power' are often subject to conceptual slippage, however, we argue that these are distinct characteristics for the contemporary television viewer. The greater choice afforded to consumers in a digital age is often assumed to equate to a more democratic media landscape. The amount of market choice is erroneously taken as disciplining the market *and* ensuring a redistribution of power. This book illustrates that, despite changing business models and technologies, power still remains with a few key players (including traditional players and FAANG[2]). It also highlights that engagement with the expanded television ecosystem requires consumers with deep pockets. Universal access and availability, however, remain integral to the public good and demonstrate the enduring significance of publicly funded media.

For us, this speaks to the intersection of digital technology with the social expectations surrounding broadcasting. Two domains where the struggle for power is likely to play out, and which will impact directly on drama production, are prominence and discoverability. Here in the UK, the Digital Economy Act (2017) compelled the regulator Ofcom to report periodically on the prominence of linear and video on demand PSB services on electronic programme guides (EPGs). In late 2018 the regulator announced a consultation on the issue and as Ofcom's content group director, Kevin Bakhurst, explains: 'We'll consider whether the traditional channels are easy to find – on tablets, TVs and smartphones – for people who value their programmes. How will viewers find them in a world that's becoming increasingly on-demand and personalised? We must consider this to ensure the PSBs are not drowned out' (Douglas 2018). Intervention by Ofcom may force Sky, Virgin Media and other pay-TV providers to ensure that on-demand content from BBC, ITV, Channel 4 and Channel 5 gets top billing on the new generation of set-top boxes and smart TVs. In our view, analyses of television drama need urgently to attend to this renewed political economy of devices and infrastructure, an area of the industry too often overlooked by television scholars.

Prominence, however, is an issue beyond the EPG, with services like Netflix and Apple embedded in the infrastructure of our viewership through deals with global television manufacturers and mobile devices. Having a dedicated button on viewers' remote controls, or an app that automatically appears on the home screen of viewers' smart TVs or mobile phone, allows services like Netflix and Apple an unprecedented

[2]FAANG refers to the five most powerful and best-performing tech stocks, namely: Facebook, Apple, Amazon, Netflix and Google.

opportunity for controlling the viewing experience and one that is unlikely to be within the financial reach of many other providers, especially smaller public service broadcasters such as S4C. As Michalis argues: 'The power and capacity to influence what can be found is not only about economic market power but, arguably more significantly, raises crucial questions about the practice of democracy' (2018, 201). To sustain public service content in the digital era will require novel approaches to content, its distribution and the audiences who access it. It is not sufficient to point to distribution portals as impartial gateways to content. Algorithms and content filtering give the perception of personalisation, yet research (Johnson 2019) demonstrates that these portals shape services and structure viewing behaviours in ways that is often imperceptible. We argue more intervention is needed to challenge normative digital logics and to ensure the visibility and easy accessibility of public service content to all audiences, though this seems to be an area that regulators seem ill-equipped to address. As television drama scholars, we regard this as an urgent area of concerns as the volume and diversity of drama that audiences enjoy today is heavily dependent on the investment by, and capacity of, indigenous public service broadcasters.

While global flows of money and international competition make it difficult for individual countries or institutions to resist this further consolidation of power within the television market, there are some tentative signs of the potential and power of collective action (Raats and Donders 2017). For example, in 2018 the European Parliament approved new regulations on streaming services like Netflix and Amazon Prime Video around the origination of their content libraries. The regulation will require that at least 30% of content carried on streaming services operating in the European Union originates from the region. Additionally, these services will be required to support the development of European productions either through direct investment or by paying into national funds. Significantly, the level of contribution in each country will be proportional to the on-demand revenues in that country, thereby attempting to offset the threat to indigenous production. Both requirements are aimed at supporting the cultural diversity and viability of the European screen sector, with similar quotas being considered in other territories such as Australia. This illustrates the need for sustained transnational collaboration to fend off the power of FAANG. However, it also reiterates the importance of geography and place within television. As we argued in Chapter 4 and again in Chapter 6, place and geography matter a great deal to drama content, and never more so than in the seemingly border-less digital age. Routine industrial elements such as geo-blocking,[3] public funding and regulation are all bound by national or supranational forces. Place, and associated elements such as language and identity, continue to be vital elements in the authenticity of drama and its value for audiences. As researchers this may require new frameworks for considering the complex mix of local and global forces at play in the television market. Therefore, an ongoing research agenda beyond the scope of this book is the particular experience of screen sectors and PSBs in smaller nations as they attempt to respond to and shape the power of global platforms (see McElroy and Noonan 2016; McElroy et al. 2018).

Why Local Production Matters in a Global Era

A key theme of this book has been the considerable potential for television drama and its production to contribute well beyond the jurisdiction of economic policy alone. For those working in the sector, for policy-makers and for audiences, local drama, and the infrastructure that produces it, is highly valued. As we argued in Chapter 2, local production fulfils a range of economic, cultural and social roles for stakeholders. This is not to imply that the products of global industries are not enjoyed and have value, however, it is the tendency for many content providers towards a dislocated drive to market dominance that is deeply problematic for us. Viewing figures for local drama testify to its enduring popularity. However, local drama does not just happen. It requires active interventions and the constant nurturing of an infrastructure including production facilities and a talent pool. It includes the maintenance of a coherent strategic focus by policy-makers, commissioning editors and other actors such as screen agencies who need to be held to account in making a production ecology in a range of locales (as indicated in Table 1.1 on sustainability). Regulators also have an important role to play in delivering plural production environments that enable rather than inhibit sustainable production. Moreover, the public good of television drama cannot be divorced from its potential to challenge social inequalities both on screen through its representational and narrative power, but

---

[3]Geoblocking is where access is restricted to certain content based on the user's geographical location gleaned from the users IP address. This is commonly used in television and film markets for copyright and licensing reasons.

also behind the screen through building a workforce that is not premised on multiple barriers and dimensions of exclusion.

As we argued at the outset, sustainability has become a much-used term in discussions of the UK's television sector despite it being a frustratingly ambiguous concept. Sustainability becomes a powerful political instrument in which growth is dependent on deregulated markets, technological innovation and transnational flows of capital. The implications are that progress is understood solely in terms of increasing national income and the accumulation of private wealth. Economic rationales operate as a proxy for all other concerns. Therefore, the concept is often instrumentalised by political decision-makers, in ways that are contradictory and limiting. The contradiction lies in the time-based qualities of the concept. Sustainability proposes long-term thinking, but often this is not achieved given changes in political direction and the very specific context of creative production in which short-term projects mitigate against medium and long-term strategising. Sustainability is deployed in an excessively limited way when it is linked to policy imperatives for attracting inward investment from global players to the neglect of indigenous production.

Sustainability is best regarded, not as a normative concept, but as a site of struggle. For instance, our research demonstrates there is a deficit within the policy landscape of a cohesive, agile and shared objective which is anchored by a deep philosophical purchase in the underlying principles of public value. Instead there is a tendency for short termism driven by a limited number of economic indicators and levers. An abundance of damning evidence pointing to structural forms of inequalities (Directors UK 2015, 2018; Kreager 2018; O'Brien et al. 2016; Saha 2012; Wing-Fai et al. 2015) and the personal testimonies of many within the industry (Huffington Post 2018) have brought to the fore the limits of the current framing of sustainability, in which unequal access to the industry remains a significant obstacle to long-term growth. Regulators, and their current terms of reference, seem ill-equipped for the challenges that this changing landscape brings or can account for the wider infrastructure and instruments that would enable public values to be preserved and reconceptualised for a digital era. For instance, a more confident approach to attribute responsibility to global players to the benefit of the development of workers at all levels is one area. If there is value in nurturing local production, policy-makers, commissioning editors and other stakeholders will need to think innovatively about the levers and initiatives needed which can overcome the binary of economic and cultural metrics.

When we talk about the sustainability of local production, embedded firmly within that is the viability of the independent production sector. Within local production ecologies indies play a major role in the sector building a critical mass of investment, employment and IP. Yet initiatives like high-end tax relief (because of its spend thresholds) rarely support the kind of local drama our research tells us is vital to the sustainability of the local ecology. Furthermore, the ability of these companies to retain and maximise the revenue stream from content rights is vital. It was favourable terms of trade which enabled them to grow and which supported local production in the first place. However, we see significant change in this area which jeopardises the sustainability of the sector; firstly, around ownership in which successful indies are swallowed up by bigger global players losing some of the autonomy and their roots to the local; there are remarkably few indies who make high-end drama in the UK *and* are truly independent.[4] Secondly, we see a threat in the relinquishing of rights to new models of commissioning like those favoured by Netflix, a change discussed in Chapter 3. Therefore, there is an outward flow of IP and few incentives to make local drama. The sustainability of the sector requires incentivising indies to take on some responsibility for the training and development of work and to think innovatively about how to do business.

There is also little connection between sustainability in its current usage and issues of social justice, economic redistribution or subjective understandings of well-being. The individual as worker or viewer is marginalised and disconnected from this conceptualisation of sustainability. Therefore, we advocate a more critical concern with the concept of sustainability and a more critical discussion of what should be protected and what is liable to extinction—to understand the winners and losers in the contemporary television production ecology. Researchers will need to expand and rethink their tools to expose normative ways of thinking

[4]Ofcom (2018, 14) defines production companies as independent if not tied to a UK broadcaster through significant common ownership. The Broadcasting (Independent Productions) Order 1991 (as amended) states that an independent producer is: (i) not employed by a broadcaster; (ii) does not have a shareholding greater than 25% in a UK broadcaster; or (iii) in which no single UK broadcaster has a shareholding greater than 25% or any two or more UK broadcasters have an aggregate shareholding greater than 50%.

within policy. Our empirical research underpins our conviction that we need to pay greater attention to the diversity and pluralism of producers and broadcasters. We argue that different visions on sustainability and how it should be measured could coexist, not only for plurality but also because different frameworks of analysis could give a better idea of the sustainability (or unsustainability) of regions, languages and identities. It is only through this more nuanced concept of sustainability that the full non-economic value of television drama can be realised and captured. In this way television drama is conceived as a public good.

References

Andersen, Mads M. T. and Vilde Schanke Sundet. 'Producing Online Youth Fiction in a Nordic Public Service Context'. Forthcoming 2019.

boyd, danah and Crawford, Kate. 'Critical Questions for Big Data'. *Information, Communication & Society* 15, 5 (2012): 662–679.

Creative Diversity Network. 'Diamond'. Accessed 18 November 2018. https://creativediversitynetwork.com/diamond/.

Directors UK. 'Adjusting the Colour Balance'. 2015. Accessed 27 October 2018. https://www.directors.uk.com/campaigns/bame-directors#previous-report.

Directors UK. 'Who's Calling the Shots?' August 2018. Accessed 31 October 2018. https://www.directors.uk.com/campaigns/gender-equality-in-uk-tv.

Douglas, Torin. 'The Battle for Prominence'. *Television Magazine*, February 2018. Accessed 6 November 2018. https://rts.org.uk/article/battle-prominence.

Forrest, David and Johnson, Beth (eds). *Social Class and Television Drama in Contemporary Britain*. Basingstoke: Palgrave Macmillan, 2017.

Huffington Post. 'Mia Kirshner and the Fight Against Workplace Sexual Harassment with #AfterMeToo'. *Huff Post* 2018. Accessed 31 October 2018. https://www.huffingtonpost.ca/2018/09/09/mia-kirshner-aftermetoo-tiff_a_23520991/.

Johnson, Catherine. *Online TV*. Abingdon, Oxon: Routledge, 2019.

Kreager, Alexis. 'Gender Inequality and Screenwriters'. *Writers Guild*, 22 May 2018. Accessed 31 October 2018. https://writersguild.org.uk/wggb_campaigns/equality-writes/.

Lotz, Amanda. *The Television Will Be Revolutionized*. 2nd edition. New York: New York University Press, 2014.

Malik, Sarita. '"Creative Diversity": UK Public Service Broadcasting After Multiculturalism'. *Popular Communication* 11 (2013): 227–241.

Malik, Sarita and Clive James Nwonka. '*Top Boy:* Cultural Verisimilitude and the Allure of Black Criminality for UK Public Service Broadcasting Drama'. *Journal of British Cinema and Television* 14, 4 (2017): 4234–444.

Max, D. T. '"SKAM," the Radical Teen Drama That Unfolds One Post At a Time'. *The New Yorker*, 18 June 2018. Accessed 7 November 2018. https://www.newyorker.com/magazine/2018/06/18/skam-the-radical-teen-drama-that-unfolds-one-post-at-a-time.

Maybin, Simon. 'The Other Big Korean Drama Right Now'. BBC, 14 June 2018. Accessed 18 November 2018. https://www.bbc.co.uk/news/business-44453310.

McElroy, Ruth and Caitriona Noonan. 'Television Drama Production in Small Nations: Mobilities in a Changing Ecology'. *Journal of Popular Television* 4, 1 (2016): 109–127.

McElroy, Ruth, Caitriona Noonan and Jakob Isak Nielsen. 'Small Is Beautiful? The Salience of Scale and Power to Three European Cultures of TV Production'. *Critical Studies in Television* 13, 2 (2018): 169–187.

Michalis, Maria. 'Distribution Dilemmas for Public Service Media: Evidence from the BBC'. In *Public Service Media in the Networked Society*, edited by Gregory Ferrell Lowe, Hilde Van den Bulck and Karen Donders, 195–210. Göteborg: Nordicom, 2018.

O'Brien, Dave, Daniel Laurison, Andrew Miles and Sam Friedman. 'Are the Creative Industries Meritocratic?: An Analysis of the 2014 British Labour Force Survey'. *Cultural Trends* 25, 2 (2016): 116–131.

Ofcom. 'Review of Regional TV Production and Programming Guidance: Consultation'. 19 December 2018. Accessed 31 March 2019. https://www.ofcom.org.uk/__data/assets/pdf_file/0015/130911/Review-of-Regional-TV-Production-and-Programming-Guidance.pdf.

Raats, Tim and Karen Donders. 'Public Service Media and Partnerships: Analysis of Policies and Strategies in Flanders'. In *Public Service Media Renewal: Adaptation to Digital Network Challenges*, edited by Michał Głowacki and Alicja Jaskiernia. Berlin: Peter Lang, 2017. https://doi.org/10.3726/978-3-653-07253-2.

Saha, Anamik. '"Beards, Scarves, Halal Meat, Terrorists, Forced Marriage": Television Industries and the Production of "Race"'. *Media, Culture & Society* 34, 4 (2012): 424–438.

Screen Australia. 'The Screen Guide: Life of Jess'. *Screen Australia*, 2018. Accessed 7 November 2018. https://www.screenaustralia.gov.au/the-screen-guide/t/life-of-jess-2018/36848.

Swinburne, Sue and Richard Fabb. 'How Web Series Are Shaking Up Australia's Screen Industry'. *The Conversation*, 30 June 2017. Accessed 7 November 2018. https://theconversation.com/how-web-series-are-shaking-up-australias-screen-industry-79844.

Wilson, Sherryl. 'In the Living Room: Second Screens and TV Audiences'. *Television and New Media* 17, 2 (2016): 174–191.

Wing-Fai, Leung, Rosalind Gill, and Keith Randle. 'Getting In, Getting On, Getting Out? Women as Career Scramblers in the UK Film and Television Industries'. *The Sociological Review* 63 (2015): 50–65.

Filmography

Black Mirror: Bandersnatch (House of Tomorrow, Netflix 2018).
Broad City (3 Arts Entertainment/Jax Media/Paper Kite Productions 2014–2019).
Butterfly (Red Production Company 2018).
Doctor Who (BBC Wales 2005–present).
Fleabag (Two Brothers Pictures 2016–present).
Game of Thrones (Home Box Office (HBO)/Television 360/Grok! Studio/ Generator Entertainment/Bighead Littlehead 2011–2019).
Killing Eve (Sid Gentle Films 2018–present).
Misfits (Clerkenwell Films 2009–2013).
Sherlock (Hartswood Films 2010–present.
SKAM (NRK 2015–2017).
Skins (Company Pictures 2007–2013).

Index

CPI Antony Rowe
Eastbourne, UK
March 09, 2020